The Year of Sluttery

A Journey of Sex, Self, and Singlehood

SCARLETT d. JONES

Scarlett d. Jones
La Que Sabe Publishing

ISBN 979-8-9923915-3-4

www.scarlettdjones.com

Snapshots dropped into my consciousness like one of those vintage Viewmaster toys.

The Hot Chef's dick in my mouth... click... his fingers pinching my nipple... click... bent over the hood of his car...

I closed my eyes and took a deep breath. A headline floated up like a dead fish, *Teacher of the Year Arrested for Public Indecency*. Oh god.

Breathe again and count this time. One, two—another headline punctured my attempt at calm, *Former Sunday School Teacher Fornicates in Public*.

Pure panic washed over me as I could now hear TMZ blaring, "Would You Want This Brazen Hussy Teaching Your Teen? Sex Video Here!"

A burst of raucous laughter from the sidewalk below snapped me back to reality. Normal Friday night sounds for downtown Kansas City. Partiers heading to John's Big Deck or The Quaff. I was used to it since I'd been living in the loft for a year now. I touched my phone to see the time, 1:18 a.m. My mind went back to the seminal moment giving me anxiety.

Well, I suppose it was semen-al if we get right down to it...

The creative force flows over the terrain of our psyches looking for the natural hollows, the arroyos, the channels that exist in us. We become its tributaries, its basins, we are its pools, ponds, streams, and sanctuaries. The wild creative force flows into whatever beds we have, those we are born with as well as those we dig with our own hands. We don't have to fill them, we only have to build them.

Women Who Run with the Wolves:
Myths and Stories of the Wild Woman Archetype
Dr. Clarissa Pinkola Estes

Contents

ACKNOWLEDGMENTS

To Seester: You've listened to too many stories, talked me into adventures when I was scared, been the receiver of the "I'm meeting this guy in case I die," photos and addresses, and let me cry on your shoulder whilst you give me wise advice. I love you always.

To my kids: Thanks for your patience and love.

To Boo: Minus your proclivity to shove weird shots at me and be mad when I throw away your blue drink in NOLA, you are the best Boo ever. Thank you for your friendship & support. Let's dance soon.

RAW Storytellers: Thank you for sharing your stories.

RAD Storytellers, especially Jamie and Lorraine, who were always there to encourage me and laugh at the slut stories in the very beginning. This would not exist without you.

To my Greater Kansas City Writing Project peeps: xoxox

Kansas City: Thank you for being home.

To the men: Thanks for the stories! And fun. ;)
Except Prince A & Baby Ginger, fuck you guys.

WARNING: MAP ISN'T GEOGRAPHICALLY CORRECT.

Cast of Characters

Baby Ginger: Porn-fucked millennial.

Boo: My millennial bestie. The cutest, sweetest, cardigan-rocking man.

Brit: Gave me a great lost condom story. First date: SoT.

Bumble Biker: Youngest man I was ever with, 33. First date: Dott Boss.

Coach: Sexy fun message game. No execution on the field. First date: HopCat in Westport.

Coffee Meets Bagel: One of those married guys. First date: Harry's in Westport.

Cranky: Gave him my whole damn summer because of his penis and compliments. First date: Afterword Tavern.

Eva: my millennial friend who looks like Eva Mendez.

Hoppy Sporty-Sport, aka Six Year Guy: Chillest man you'd ever meet, named for his love of beer & TV sports. First date: The Roost.

Liberal Marine: A sugarface. His dog stuck its nose in my bumholio once. First date: Harry's at River Market.

Married Guy: First (and only) date: Harry's, Westport.

Masseuse: A Zaddy. First date: yoga class at his house.

Prince A: A fuckin' asshole with a gorgeous piercing in his penis. First date: The Peanut, downtown.

Seester: Baby sister. She supports me, listens to all my bullshit.

Sexy Lips: The one who likes to say "creamed." First sex in the year of sluttery. First date: Downbeat Coffee, Westport.

Tantric Man: Taut everywhere. First date: Parlor, Crossroads.

The Audacious Bitch: My rebellious side that makes me more fun.

The DJ: A gentleman in the streets, a strumpet in the sheets. First date: John's Big Deck.

The Vexed Hillbilly: Married to him for 28 years. Raccoon hunter and Budweiser drinker. First date: his parents' couch.

The Hot Chef: Poly. Sweet as pie. First date: My loft.

The Poet: Smart-as-fuck sex machine. First date: Julep, Westport.

Trivia Man: First man I ever gave my number to. First date: his hot tub.

Zen Man: Come to find out he wasn't very zen. First date: SoT.

Timeline

1984-2013 Before Sluttery. The Vexed Hillbilly Decades.

2013-2019 Before Sluttery. Hoppy Sporty-Sport.

2019-2020 The Year of Sluttery.

2020-2021 The Year of Discovery.

2021-2022 The Year of The Wild Woman.

2022-2023 The Year of The Bad Bitch.

2023-2024 The Year of Abandon.

2024-2025 The Year of Transformation.

2025-2026 The Year of Abundance.

Mary Fucking Tyler Moore

April 2019

If you're over the age of half a hundred, you may remember *The Mary Tyler Moore Show*. Opening credits, Mary is in the BIG CITY now. She looks up at the skyline with her signature toothy smile and spins, throwing her hat up in the air. She doesn't care who sees it. She's fuckin' happy to be out of small town USA and in the BIG CITY. I loved that show so much.

If my parents knew how that show would influence me, I'm betting they'd have turned the channel back to *Little House on the Prairie* and *The Waltons*. Seriously, think about the values promoted by Mary Tyler Moore versus the family shows. It was the fuckin' 70's. The Help Wanted column still was headed with Jobs for Women, Jobs for Men. I ain't kiddin'. And here's this lady who thinks she can make it on her own? Mm mmm mm.

I was watching that show in very formative years, elementary through middle school but I just realized how very much I wanted to BE Mary Tyler Moore. I have had that idea, that icon, that touchstone, in my mind, nay, my soul, for over 40 years. And yet I just got there, where I wanted to be this whole time. But we'll get to that in a minute. We gotta back up so you can see how wild it is that I'm becoming Mary Fucking Tyler Moore.

That little girl watching that show back in the 70s? She was sitting smack dab in the middle of a 400-acre beef cattle farm over five miles from Small Town, Missouri. Five miles is a lot for someone who is not allowed to ride her bike out of her mother's eyesight. Five miles is a lot when your mom got her driver's license at the age of 30 because why would she need it before that? Five miles is a lot when your parents' whole existence is that farm and they don't go to ball games or church or none 'o that stuff. It was a beautiful safe way to grow up. I climbed trees, played with sticks, skipped rocks, and tormented my baby sisters. We chased cows and baled hay and learned to drive the tractor. You are beginning to see how far Mary is from every minute of my daily life. How foreign. And yet she stuck in there, way deep in there.

At school I'm channeling Mary: Student Council secretary, National Honor Society officer, Math League, newspaper staff and... president of the Future Homemakers of America. Now that's not very Mary Tyler Moore-y you are probably thinking. I mean, Homemakers? Now it is called FACS, family and consumer sciences. Cuz no one ain't wanting to be a homemaker. Hell, I was president of Future Homemakers and I didn't want to be a homemaker.

Our town's claim to fame was Paul Harvey had recently mentioned us on his national radio show because we had the highest per capita teen pregnancy rate in the country. No boys wanted to date this career-minded feminist in rural Missouri, until a good ol' boy noticed me, a former captain of the football team. No way, the captain of the football team wants to go on a date with me?

I didn't think about the fact that he'd been a big deal when he was in school… three years before. I didn't think about the fact that three years after graduation he was still cruising the loop in our small town, working full time, and living at home where his mommy was still picking his underwear up off the floor. I put him right up on a pedestal and lost my MTM card. Wow he liked me! Put aside everything.

At home my parents went into full-on fear mode that the big bad world is going to hurt me and holy hell she's dating a hillbilly. They clamped down which makes an 18-year-old settle right down and do what you want doesn't it? Nah it doesn't. It makes you wilder and strain more toward the thing they don't want you to do.

Now I can see why they were freaking out. But then, nope. I married The Vexed Hillbilly to escape their rules even though I'd escaped to college. He got a ring on it before I realized. Nobody was building me up. Nobody saw who I really was and encouraged me. In their defense, I didn't even know myself because I was 19 years old. Not a great time to make lifetime decisions.

I lost Mary and I went very far away from her for 25 years. Marriage was devastating. Just a few months after walking down the aisle, I realized it was a mistake immediately. In year two, he yelled at me for buying a $1 whisk. Granted with inflation that would be $5 today, but still. I also learned he didn't like shenanigans of any sort. We'd just planted some flowers outside our new trailer home located on his parent's farm. I squirted him with the hose, thinking it would be like the movies. He was supposed to grab the hose and squirt me, then we would get all sexy steamy. Instead he exploded in anger, yelled at me, and stomped away.

In year three, I left The Vexed Hillbilly but then a Southern Baptist "counselor" pastor told me I'd made a promise to God so I went back for 25 more years.

I became fully immersed in the Southern Baptist church: Sunday School teacher, youth worker, choir, church nursery, Vacation Bible School teacher, you name it. I was listening to sermons about how wives should remain under the umbrella of the authority of our husbands so that if anything bad came down the pike we'd be protected. What the fuck logic is that?

I birthed three kids whom I love with my whole heart. I became a teacher. I've had the privilege to teach over 2000 young people. Mary was always there, although she had a potty mouth.

In 2009, I went through the National Writing Project's Summer Institute. I began writing down my thoughts and my dreams. And I began to think of divorce. It took four years but I wrote my way out of the marriage and left The Vexed Hillbilly.

I was living in Springfield, Missouri until my son graduated from high school which is not a BIG CITY at all. But I was running, I had decorated my house so cute. I was writing. I wanted to flirt and have some sex already. At dinner one night I asked two girlfriends how to meet people, just go up to men in the grocery store? The gym? What the hell...

"Plenty O' fish.com," said one.

"Noooo!" said the other and told me how awful it was.

I downloaded it immediately when I got home. I chose Hoppy Sporty Sport for my first date, because he asked, and he was funny. We were not impressed with each other on the first date, but the second date was at his house. When he came to answer the door in that backward baseball cap and gym shorts... honey, I was done. I never went out with anyone else. I fell hard—so hard.

In case you missed that: two months after leaving my 28-year-marriage I went on a first date and stayed with him for six years. What the ever living hell. I put him up on a goddamn pedestal because he was ten years younger than me and so cute. You know, tall but not too thin, a former redhead who grayed up in a good way and he's kind (and he had a drinking problem and perhaps he was depressed).

When I look back at my "decision making process" I'm amazed at how I haven't put myself on a pedestal, only everyone else. I'm glad I have those three complicated intricate adult children, god I love them. Without them it might hurt a lot more to think of all the years I missed out on living my Mary dreams. But here I am. I'm leaning in. I'm beginning to see that I was always her. I'm living in the BIG CITY. I walk around and take photos of the buildings. I have a posse of Rhodas and Murrays. I ate Easter brunch by myself at a sidewalk table near the River Market and I am happy. I am working on keeping that balance, keeping who I am, figuring out who I am and enjoying the hell out of all of it.

I've learned that no one is worth losing Mary.

I don't ever want to lose her now.

Launching Out

April 2019

I 'm from the Ozarks where we don't hire fancy movers. On moving day your friends show up with a stock trailer or pickup truck, having cleaned out the cow shit with a garden hose and broom the day before. But this move was taking place in the metropolis of Kansas City. I was leaving my dream house, the looks-like-it-belongs-in-a-fairy-tale brick Tudor and the man I'd bought it with, Hoppy Sporty Sport, (so named for his love of beer and television sports) to a loft where I'd be living solo for the first time in my life. Even though Kansas City was historically a cow town, my friends owned nary a cow nor a stock trailer and there was no way all my stuff would fit in their SUVs so I rented a Uhaul to move my stuff.

I had found the loft a month before in the Kansas City Library District. There were benches that looked like stacks of books; a statue of Mark Twain, legs crossed, patiently waiting for you to cop a squat beside him; and a chandelier-bedecked library inside a 100-

year-old former bank building. The pièce de résistance were the 25-foot book spines painted on the side of the library parking garage, a whole city block of these colorful gargantuan book spines. My friends and I followed the rental agent into the second floor apartment of the appropriately named Library Lofts. The eight-foot windows burst with views of the book spines, namely *To Kill a Mockingbird, Invisible Man,* and *Lord of the Rings.* Voracious readers all, we looked at each other in glee.

"I can just see you sitting here writing," said one friend as she peered out the window.

"What is this for?" the other friend's son exclaimed, twirling with his arms out in the huge walk-in closet.

I had to have it. I knew I belonged there. After a bit of paperwork, we headed to lunch at the nearby River Market, the spring sun warming us as we celebrated. I'd be moving Easter weekend, merely a month later. Life as I knew it would never be the same.

Thus began 30 days of packing, building a wall of tear-stained boxes in the dining room that Hoppy couldn't ignore. Instead of our wedding, I had planned a move, one that would end our story of six years. The beginning of that end had come eight months before in the dog days of Missouri summer…

I put a hand over my eyes so I could see Hoppy through the glare of the July sun as I prepared to ask the question that was burning my gut. A few hours before my hairstylist/friend had asked me what was going on with the proposal. I'd shrugged and said, "Nothing." She was asking because of course she was up to date on all things romantic in my life, as I was hers.

Hoppy and I had talked about getting engaged that year because we'd been together five years, lived together three years, and had moved from the Ozarks to buy a home together in Kansas City. If we were gonna get married, and we'd said we were gonna, it was time. I wanted to be proposed to even though it seemed a little silly.[1] Now it was the end of July, seven months into 2018, and I'd asked that he not do a holiday engagement so there were just a few months left. It had been in the back of my mind, especially the week before when we were flying through the air on a parasail in Seattle thinking how cool it would be to get engaged with our feet dangling hundreds of feet above Puget Sound. But as I sat there in her kitchen, grays disappearing under the dye I somehow knew without a doubt, nothing was happening with the proposal. I also knew I'd have to ask him about it when I got home.

We were sitting on the deck talking about what to cook for dinner while I gathered my courage to ask.

He said, "Well, I'm going to mow the lawn," and stood up. He took care of the lawn like he did everything in his life, responsibly and timely. I'd learned from him to rinse out the coffee pot after every use, not to use serrated knives to cut vegetables, and pillows were to be placed in their slips with the tag hanging out.

"Uh, just a second," I said. Something in me was so scared but I didn't know why. I took him in, standing there patiently in the Thanksgiving 5K shirt we'd gotten after we ran it together. I'd always found him incredibly attractive, his kind blue eyes almost always twinkling with humor, mouth that usually wore a smirk as he was getting ready to tease me about something, his tall lanky body with no ass, his perfectly-shaped hands with lean

---

[1] This was partly because I didn't get the cool proposal from The Vexed Hillbilly just something like, "We're gonna get married, right?" post-coitus on my freshman dorm bed.

fingers. I even loved the bump on his wrist and the sprinkling of ginger hairs on his chest. I'd fallen head over heels for him on our second date, a mere two months after I'd left my 28-year marriage with The Vexed Hillbilly. Even though he drank more than I liked, every single day to be exact, and I wished he wanted to have more sex, once a week wasn't enough for me, I was still crazy in love with him.

He tilted his head at my silence, "What's up?"

"Um, so I was wondering about the proposal thing?" sitting very still as if waiting for impact.

It came.

"Oh," he said. A few beats of silence stretched out. A few seconds that felt like hours, "I forgot about that."

"You forgot about it?" I stammered.

He sat back down but didn't say anything.

"What's going on?" I asked. "Do you want to get married?"

"I don't know," he finally said.

"You don't know..." My eyes counted the bricks behind his head. I could see the kitchen where we cooked together. Beyond that was the dining room with the bowl of funny masks we'd bought at the Goodwill Outlet. Many photos had been taken using them with friends and family laughing at their images in the wall-sized mirror. Turn the corner and there was the living room where we watched WWE every Monday.

"Do you still want to be together until we die?" I asked.

"Yes," he answered quickly. "I love you."

"Ummm okay," I said, thinking to break down all the parts of marriage to help him say words. "Would you get me a pretty ring to show I'm yours?"

"Yes," he even smiled.

Huh. Okay. Next thing. "Uh, can we have a party to

celebrate that we want to be together forever?"

"Sure."

Okay he loved me, wanted to be with me, would give me a ring I could wear on the third finger of my left hand, and we could have a reception. What was the problem? Money?

"Would you put me on your accounts?" He had no kids, and his family was loaded. As a single mom public school teacher, I very definitely wasn't.

"Yes."

I was stuck. I couldn't think of one other thing that was marriage other than a commitment, a ring, a party, and legal stuff.

"Well then what is it?" I asked.

"Don't take offense," he said. "But I don't want to be divorced. I think it is pathetic"

I heard him say it but I couldn't wade through the meaning of it. The vexing "Don't take offense" phrase always means you will take offense, then the idea that we'd get divorced, then the word "pathetic" hung in the air. I was divorced. He was saying I was pathetic?

"Don't take offense to this," I said. "But I think it is much more pathetic to be a never-married 44-year-old man." Then I walked into the house upstairs to the bedroom, locked the door and sobbed. We moved around each other for a few days silently. I thought about all he had said and realized I didn't care so much about being married. The problem was that he had not communicated that he didn't want to be married. We sat down to talk it through. I asked him to do three things: go to couple counseling to help the communication problem, not drink every single day for his mental and physical health, and to go to the doctor for a testosterone check to help with our sex life. He agreed. In the next few months I found a counselor. He made it to two counseling sessions, then quit coming. He didn't even attempt the other two requests. I kept going to counseling and figured out that even though I loved him, and even though he was a good person, it wasn't going to work.

Eight months after the "forgotten proposal," it was moving day. A passel[2] of friends showed up to help. When the 15-foot-long truck was full of my former lives. I hopped in and drove it sixty-four blocks north to the Library Lofts with some bad bitch energy from my decades of driving farm trucks. When the Uhaul was empty, I handed out thank you's: booze to the millennial guys, Elle concert tickets to my millennial girlfriends, thank you cards for my Gen X girlfriends.[3] Hugs and congratulations were exchanged, then I was alone. The past eight months of counseling, making the decision to leave, preparing to leave, and talking about leaving had torn me to shreds. I had made it through the gauntlet and now this 750-square-space was all mine. Excited to put my new home together, I began unpacking.

xoxoxo

This was my first place to live solo. Ever. No man, no kids, not even a pet. I put the baker's rack by the windows, placing plants, twinkle lights, and one of my beloved antique typewriters on it. I put together the vintage Ikea bookshelves, filling them with my books and oddities: a paper mache skull, the miniature diver helmet, the mayo jar of old keys. By the time I had everything the way I wanted, the weekend had flown by.

---

[2] Ozarks-speak for "a bunch."

[3] This is BS. I owe the Gen-Xers some booze or tix. I am aware.

21

I decided I'd give the dating apps a try. I left Hoppy Sporty-Sport on Good Friday and had a Bumble account by 10 p.m. on Easter Sunday, resurrecting my dating life. Enough crying. Time for some fun.

I had heard that Bumble was women-owned, so Bumble it was. I uploaded some cute pictures and wrote my bio, mentioning that I adored kissing and cursing. I found out the woman has to make the first move. It was more work than I thought it would be, trying to be funny and interesting. I messaged the first guy I matched with that the Crapola sign behind his head was funny. He informed me snottily that it was a real company. No sense of humor. Goodbye. The second match told me that my beloved Seattle, where my oldest lived and I hoped to move to someday, was a dead place and only Portland was good. Dead? WTF. Unmatch. So far this wasn't much fun.

My middle daughter came over on Monday night to help me put my bed together. I told her about joining Bumble. She was a bit mean, saying things like, "You can't be without a man for three days?" and "All you are gonna meet are weirdos, people with diseases," and something else I've blocked out entirely.[4] She left and I felt shitty. I deleted the app and let her know. I trusted my daughters. They were wise about dating whereas I knew nothing.

A few hours later, I was getting ready for bed. And I have this rebellious side who doesn't like being told what to do. She's an Audacious Bitch.

So... I looked for other dating apps.

I found one called HUD, Hook-Up Dating.

Hook.

Up.

---

4 These are all valid points.

Dating.

Of course, I downloaded it immediately. Within 30 seconds a message popped up. From a 31-year-old. (cough, 23 years younger)

Hey what's up, he messaged.

Not much, you? (Shakespeare I know.)

Wanna have some fun?

I stared at the phone. I don't know, did I? What did "fun" even mean?

A video of him jerking off popped into the chat. It was a nice healthy-sized member. Fascinated, I watched it a couple of times. I'd never done this whole sexting thing. It hadn't come up much when I was a Sunday School teacher and all.

I thought, what the hell? Life number three. Go.

I lifted my shirt and sent a booby shot. He liked it.

I sent a pic of my fingers, diddling around.

He liked it.

Oh yeah. Great pussy. You enjoying that?

Yes I am.

I decided to go for the gusto. I put on the black lace nightie Hoppy had never liked and grabbed my trusty purple vibrator. I took a video of me using... I should name the vibrator. That's a thing, right? I decided on Don. Yes Don, as in Don Fucking Draper baby.[5] I sent the video.

He lost his shit, then told me how sexy I was. I sent another. I felt sexy. I looked sexy in the video, which did not show my face by the way. I was that smart at least. I'd never done this. It was more fun than I would have thought.

You have Kik? he messaged.

No. What the fuck is Kik?

---

[5] Hello Jon Hamm. We are both from Missouri. Wanna grab a cocktail?

You have any video chat?

Ummm Google Duo?

I quickly downloaded Kik because I realized Google Duo had my email with my real name in it. I didn't want the owner of said dick to have my real name. A little blue bubble popped up on the screen. What the hell was this? I poked it. Although it was dark, I could see that he was in a truck.

"Are you driving?" I asked, peering into my phone screen.

"Yes I'm driving home."

I stared at his shadowy silhouette, headlights passing, lighting his face up every few seconds, a stranger I'd just bared all to. My brain felt like it was slogging through fog. The dick video from just a few minutes before had been in a homey bathroom but here he was, driving. All of a sudden it was all so real.

"Driving home? Where were you?" I asked.

"Out with my buddies at a bar."

"But the video you sent from your bathroom?" The fog cleared. "Oh… you had it saved?"

"Yeah, don't you have one saved?" He laughed.

"Uhhhhhh…. No."

Was I supposed to? Is that a thing I'm supposed to have? That seemed like a trick. If I was going to have video sex, it seemed like something to do in the moment.

"Well why don't you have some more fun while I watch?"

Then another thought came slamming in. He had been with his "buddies at a bar" the last hour. I was now seeing it clearly in my mind, the phone being passed around the bar. On my first weekend of being single, my coochie, my lady parts, my vajayjay had been shown around a bar in Kansas City. It ain't that big of a city. Forget wading in, I had cannonballed into the dating pool.

"Use that thing again so I can see it," he pressed.

"I already did," I said in a monotone. Now I had pictures in my head of Don Draper going in and out, in and out.

"Show me some more of that gorgeous pussy," he wheedled.

"Nah, this feels strange to me," I said.

"Here, I will pull over and do me while you do you," he said, all in a rush not to lose me. Too late. I hung up. Deleted the app. Deleted all the videos.

After I watched them again.

I looked good, bitches.

Moral of the story: If you are sexting keep it in mind that they might be out and about and for damn sure, keep your face out of it.

xoxoxo

Let's be honest. I did feel empowered from the Hook-Up Dating experience, but I did not want to do it again any time soon. I went back to Bumble the next day, daughter's derision be damned.

I began talking to a man who was close to my age, could write a sentence, and looked cute in his pictures, so I sent him my number. We talked of travel, life, and sex. Well… he talked about sex.[6] We set up a happy hour date for the next day. That morning I was heading out for some errands when he said he was thinking of heading down to Westport, the errand neighborhood,

---

6 Red flag number one. If a dude talks about sex the first day, the date won't actually be fun because his blood is all in his penis instead of his brain.

just to see me.[7] A warning bell went off. I brushed it off and said happy hour would be good, completed my tasks, headed home, showered, and got ready for my first first date in six years.[8] I was nervous but thought I looked pretty good with my red floral blouse paired with the push-up bra showing a teasing amount of cleavage, new jeans, and my chunky heels. I threw on my olive green Gap jacket from Goodwill to counteract the sexy vibe since it was 4 p.m. in the afternoon. I gave myself a little pep talk and headed out. I had chosen a sports bar called Beer 30 to meet at since it was a few blocks from where I lived. I'd never been there and hated the name but it was convenient. I texted I was out front. He texted back, *I see you.*

I turned around and my heart sank.

He did not look like his photos. At. All.

Oh, the photos were of him. A much, much younger him.

On Bumble he was a professor-ish man with short gray hair, cute, age 54. This guy was 65 if he was a day. A not-cute-Einstein sort of look. His forehead had eaten his hair back to the middle of his head where five-inch gray locks bounced as he walked toward me. He was smiling with all his teeth at me.

I immediately wanted to run away. But I didn't know how.

He held the door open for me. A cavernous bar with silent unblinking TVs greeted me. I felt the pull to leave, to be home with my feet up reading my book. I told myself he deserved a nice time since his work was

---

7 Red flag number two. Wayyyy too eager, which means he is desperate.

8 It was also my second "first date" in 35 years but that's difficult to write. For so many reasons.

something that made the world a better place to live, and he even volunteered. Hell, he was reading to children right after our meetup. Also, I could see his excitement to meet me. My ego loved it. I decided I'd stay for a half hour.[9]

He led me upstairs. The only other people in the place besides us were a bartender and a security guy. I got a whiskey diet, he ordered a light beer. I pulled out a bar stool to sit down, but he had picked up our drinks and headed to a couch in front of a huge TV setup, for gaming. Little did I know the games were about to begin. He stepped back for me to sit first. I made the mistake of sitting in the corner of the couch. He plunked himself down right in my personal space, setting our drinks on the coffee table. I reached for the whiskey diet like a security blanket, or maybe a chastity belt. Clasping the thin plastic carefully I took a drink. I suppose it was a bit early for whiskey but I was damn glad I had it to calm my nerves. He didn't pick up his drink, turning toward me instead.

He looked at me like I was Angelina Jolie.

Like I was a steak and potato meal for a condemned man.

Like I was the breast to a hungry baby.

The Audacious Bitch began to stir inside me. She is rebellious and also very curious. Sometimes I can actually feel myself stepping back to observe what shit is about to go down as she steps forward in glee. She has gotten me in trouble many times through the years, proceeding when the logical side of me was saying, "Bail! Now!" Because of her, I had a tattoo on my foot from a Girls' night out with the First Baptist ladies in the metropolis of Springfield, Missouri. We'd been

---

9   Isn't it funny that I felt like I needed to reward this good-doing? Like it was my job to say good boy.

drinking (shhhh don't tell) and saw the tattoo shop across the street from the bar we just left, so we'd filed in to look around. I wanted to be the coolest person so I got one of the dumbest tattoos one can get, the Kanji Japanese symbol for "believe," a nod to Jesus you know. Years later I got it covered up with a big flower.

The Audacious Bitch was in charge again now as I was fascinated by the situation I found myself in, on a date with a man I was not attracted to who was getting ready to make his moves in an empty sports bar. Everything in me wanted to go home, but what moves might he make? I stayed to see what was going to happen. I had no voice to say no anyway. I'd been raised to be a nice girl, don't make a fuss, go along to get along. Put others before yourself and all that shit.

He was just smiling and finding out about me and wanted to marry me. He didn't say that, but I could see it in his eyes. He just kept laughing at his good fortune. He flung his arm toward me to give me a hug and knocked my drink, spilling it on me. He apologized profusely and then grabbed toward me a little more gently.

We kissed. And then kissed more. And tongues were involved. I kept thinking, "Okay if I close my eyes, you know, it's not so bad. I can do this." We made out, full on, in an empty sports bar at 4:fucking 30. I knew the bartender was watching us and it made me nervous. We were still the only people in the place. We made out more and he smiled more and professed his love with his eyes and laugh. He literally could not believe his luck. I couldn't believe his luck either.

I moved back from a long kiss and saw the bartender and a bouncer standing near us. Perhaps they were checking to see if I'd been roofied.

"I have to go," he said, his whole body slumping,

looking at me with puppy dog eyes.

I told him again how nice it was that he volunteered. He asked if I stayed up late. I said no.

We walked to the stairs where he pushed me against the wall and we kissed more. He went for second base and I let him. He touched my nipples through my shirt and it was pretty nice. My logical side was screaming at me at this point to stop. Audacious Bitch was laughing her ass off. He had been super sexual in his texts so I suppose I should have been ready but I had developed no defenses for this onslaught. Also, I was still trying to get past his looks that I'd never have swiped right on. In his defense, I never said to stop but he never asked to do the things he was doing either.

I was ready to go, so happy that he had this volunteering appointment so I didn't have to say that. I wondered what the bartenders thought and I was embarrassed.

We walked out. He mourned that he had plans all weekend with his children, hugged me, and walked away. A text popped up immediately telling me how wonderful I was.

He texted me a booty call at 9:30 but I ignored it. I ghosted him because I didn't know what to say. I unmatched on Bumble and blocked his phone.

Oh also… if you're in the KC area, he's still on the apps.

If you see a professorish dude with cute curly gray hair and a kayak, swipe left, unless of course you like liars and PDA, then obviously it's a right swipe.

xoxoxo

Sexy Lips and I matched Wednesday night, right after the Einstein debacle.

I opened with: *I must say that you are pretty cute, if your pix are real. I am new to this and met someone today who had used 10-year-old pictures in their bio.*

My pix are all in the past 18 months. :) and thank you. Can we have tea soon? Not big on getting to know someone on text, he messaged back.

Tea? Yes. I hate the text thing also. I'm dropping this app because it's annoying and I'm just gonna live my awesome life, but tea and conversation would be nice.[10]

All the next day, I kept checking my phone. He hadn't messaged back so I started talking to a new match, Coach.

Finally that night, Sexy Lips got back with me, which felt like eons. Between the soul-killing marriage to The Vexed Hillbilly and Hoppy's low sex drive, I didn't want to waste a minute. I was ready to try new things, meet new people. I chose Downbeat Coffee & Tea, a cute place in an old house in Westport, for the tea date.

I got there early and talked with the owner before he arrived. I gave her all the details of the forgotten proposal and three dates in my first week of being single.[11] She told me I was doing things right. Another customer came in so I went in the other room and milled around. I set my stuff by a little table instead of the cute couch by the window because I was still having some PTSD from Einstein and that couch. I rifled through the stack of books to get my mind off my nervousness and sat down with *Eat, Pray, Love* to re-read the good part, the Italy chapter, of course.

Sexy Lips arrived. We hugged. I liked his vibe.

---

10 Bahahahahaha, It took over two years to drop the apps. Okay, okay, you got me. I haven't dropped them. It's like a drug I go back to, less and less, but still.

11 I tell everyone all the details all the time. Open book. Storyteller.

Maybe because he looked like his pix.

We went up to order together. He said, "Oh I'll buy since you had to drive."

I didn't know this would be a negotiation, had assumed he would be paying. For one, he had asked me. Two, it was tea for pete's sake, around $10. Three, he made more money than I did, a lot more, like $100,000 more.

We got our chai lattes. He said, "Let's sit on the couch."

He touched my fingers and complimented my nails. They were awful looking. I had pulled all the shellac off. He said they were naturally feminine, which honestly is a concern because if I want fecking bright green on my nails I shall have it. We talked about music, writing, then marijuana, deciding he would show me the ways since I'd had so few experiences with it.

The other couple left. We were alone. We leaned forward at the same time and kissed the softest nicest kiss. He did that lovely thing where the man puts his hands on your face. I felt noticed. I felt seen. The kissing was hot. He was slow. I felt like I was trying to rush it, but he stayed slow, which helped me to slow down. We kissed for a full five minutes.

Beep! Beep! Beep!

The timer on my phone went off. The Audacious Bitch had thought it would be a fun challenge to set up back to back dates. I had to go meet Coach. I had told Sexy Lips I had until 4:30 because I was meeting friends. A white lie.

We made a plan to hang out again soon.

At his place.

xoxoxo

After we matched I messaged Coach, *Okay, your answers are funny as fuck. BUT you only have one picture and you didn't write a bio*[12]*. I like to read the little paragraphs. Also I recently met a dude who posted a 10-year-old pic so I guess that's a thing?*

I can assure you that my picture is not 10 years old. I simply don't take a lot of photos, he messaged back.

He wrote his little paragraph and it was pretty good.

He then asked: *If I may be so bold as to ask, what exactly is 'sexy time'?*

I had answered the Bumble question of what three things a good relationship needs with, "Honesty, laughter and good sexy time."

He explained that some women think sexy time meant him running a vacuum cleaner, which is sexy you have to admit. I said good sexy time could mean lots of things. I didn't tell him I had put that because I hadn't had much sex the last few years. Hoppy and I had fallen into a 15-minutes-on-Sunday morning routine that wasn't enough for me. The irony was that I'd had a similar arrangement, (sex on Wednesday and Sunday, church days) for several years with The Vexed Hillbilly who was the most oversexed person I'd ever met. I'd gone from being with someone I didn't even like who got turned on if I wore shorts, to someone I loved who didn't bat an eye if I walked naked through the room. My goal now was to find someone I liked who also liked sex.

When Coach said he had a lifetime supply of Viagra and I countered with it being good he had his priorities in order, he said: *Boy Scout motto— always be prepared.*

I vollied with: *Good motto. Mine is to grab life by the balls.*

He replied: *Could you possibly change that to cuddle gently*

---

12 Red Flag. Now I will not swipe right on someone if they can't take a moment to write a few sentences.

He perhaps wasn't as funny as I first thought. The bar was pretty low because most Bumble dudes seemed kinda boring and either started immediately talking about sex or weren't flirty at all. Coach had this funny way of approaching it where he tried to get me to coax him. Pretty clever. We made a plan to meet.

To his query if ravaging would happen I responded, *Ravaging might happen… if you aren't 80.*

What if I am 56 and strikingly handsome? He texted.

What if I am 54 and a bit squishy in the middle? I texted.

Well, squishy people are usually easier to catch. Besides, at 80 I'm just glad somebody will go out with me!

I might let you catch me. We shall see. Looking forward to the chase, I responded.

Don't make me expend too much energy. I'll need it for other things.

Note to self: only a saunter.

Note to self: walk a little faster than a saunter, he said.

I was very attracted to that sense of humor and excited to meet him. I drove to our meeting place, a bar called Hopcat in Westport, less than a mile from where I'd just met Sexy Lips so I probably still had a bit of whisker burn. I was waiting at the light to turn left and saw him waiting out front on the sidewalk. My heart sank.

He was wearing the requisite older white man uniform which never failed to channel The Vexed Hillbilly and his ilk. A buttoned up golf shirt on top, big white running shoes on bottom. Between his tall white crew socks and loose khaki shorts with lots of pockets a bit of pale leg showed. Nooooooooooo. I had wanted him to look better than his picture.[13] I sat there at the

---

13 I had not learned yet that this rarely happens. In fact the Einstein situation of shaving age and pounds is the norm.

light just staring at him. For half a second I thought of driving home but I could never do that. It's clothes; those are changeable. Right?

He told me to order whatever I wanted, he was getting it. He put his head in his hands and shook it when he found out it was my first week on online dating. He said things like when it's over for a woman it's over; a man can move heaven and earth and it won't help. He told me I was doing things right by finding my own way. He was closed minded in some things he said about music and my decision to go back to school to be a therapist. It sounded like 80s rock were the quintessential tunes everyone should love and that therapy was unnecessary.

He asked me to dinner. When I accepted, he asked what my favorite kind of food was. To my answer of Italian, he asked if I'd been to Anthony's, a Kansas City institution that used to be owned by the mob. I had not, so off we went. We dropped my vehicle at my loft and I hopped in his truck.

During dinner he stopped talking and just ate. I wasn't sure if he'd run out of things to talk about or if he doesn't like to talk while he eats. He wanted to pay for everything; I let him. I loved his sense of humor, hated his sense of fashion and some of his opinions but thought it would be worth a second date if he were a good kisser.

After dinner, I followed him to his side of the truck. It completely unnerved him. He'd been all, "You will ravage me," on text but now that I actually wanted to ravage him he seemed scared.

He stammered, "What are you doing?"

I said, "I'm going to kiss you." And I did.

And it was like kissing a wall.

Fuck.[14]

I went back around to my side and hopped in. He pulled up in front of my place and I leaned in, another wall kiss. Damnit.

I've barely talked to him since. I have friends. I don't know what I want from him. Do you always feel an attraction right off? I feel like you would.

It's hard not to want to befriend the world.

xoxoxo

Sexy Lips and I set our second date for his home on a Wednesday afternoon. He said he had wine but if I was picky I could bring some. I said I wasn't picky, but I'd bring some if he liked. He said he appreciated my "straightforwardness."

We set up the date but didn't do any of the normal, "How's your day going?" texts the days before.

Wednesday came and I was so nervous that I had stomach pains. Needless to say this is not sexy. It bothered me all day at work. I was popping Immodium AD like it was Chiclets. I didn't want to cancel. I had the idea that I would feel better once I got there. The Audacious Bitch and I wanted to get laid, so off we went to his place for an after-school special.

He lived in a gorgeous hundred-year-old house, a bit messy but not unclean. He kissed me and I felt better. We sat on the couch and kissed. And kissed and kissed. He was good at it, soft lips, sensuous and slow.

We smoked CBD. We talked. He asked me if I wanted to have sex. I said yes. He led me upstairs to his bedroom. I took off my shirt, shoes, and pants. The

---

14 I know now that he was probably nervous, so nervous. He may have been a better kisser on date two, but our vibes were more friend than anything.

movies always get this part wrong, leaving out the awkwardness of bending over to take off your socks, pulling tight jeans from curvy thighs. I was standing there in my bra and cute undies. He removed them and just stared. He was standing there in a t-shirt, boxers and socks, just silent. I died a little inside. He knew I was not confident because I had told him that I was "squishy in the middle." He was squishy in the middle just as much as me or more. I always forget that many men have a better depiction of themselves while most women I know are constantly picking ourselves apart. No more texting people that I'm "squishy in the middle."

So… the sex. Interesting. He finally took off his t-shirt and underwear, left his damn socks on, and jumped right in. He made a quick pass at the nipples but not enough, not remotely enough, and that was it for foreplay besides poking at me with his dick to get hard after we got in bed. I was hoping for some fooling around beforehand. I was wondering if he knew about foreplay. How could he not know women need 20 minutes to get warmed up? What about this important bit called the clit-or-is? Dude. Learn her, find her, be kind to her. After a bit of poking he asked me to suck his balls. I said okay. They just appeared above my head, dangling there. I did my best but wondered if I'd get to be on the receiving end. Not that day apparently.

He said he liked to do it slow. No kidding. If he'd been bigger it might have been mind-blowing. It was better than wham-bam-thank-you-ma'am. My leg started falling asleep. It was kind of zen but I hadn't had sex in a while and I needed it but I wanted more, more movement, more biting, more passion.

While we were having sex he made funny noises. I understand each to his own and you get into the sex and all but it was unnerving and hard to stay hot when he's whimpering like a baby throughout.

He asked if I "creamed."[15] I lied.

He warned me that he was loud when he "creamed." No kidding. He bawled loudly like a moose. Like four times. He asked if I would give future blow jobs and I said yes. I did not ask if he would go down on me but tit for tat.

Afterward he made me spaghetti. We drank my wine, smoked more CBD, listened to music, talked, and laughed. I think I will go back again.

p.s. I left my favorite ring there damnit. Don't wear jewelry you love to go fuck.

---

15 I think this is icky, do you? "Creamed?" It just makes me feel icky, like cream cheese or something. Gross.

On a Roll

May 2019

It had been less than two weeks since I'd left Hoppy and become officially single. 54 years of life was behind me but what was ahead? The Audacious Bitch had been in fine form, pushing me out of my comfort zone. I'd exposed myself on the Hook-Up Dating video date, had my nipples awakened by Einstein, been disappointed by Coach's wall kiss, and gotten laid by Sexy Lips. I'd learned that people use old photos, that a guy could be so damn cool in messaging but not as vibrant in real life, and that I was going to have to learn to have a voice in the bedroom if I was going to enjoy it. The nice girl who always put others first would need to die. The idea made me cringe inside. I didn't know how to be anything else.

I was also beginning to see what I liked. I wanted to take pieces of each of the three dates I had the first week and then throw another type of man in there to make it good. I wanted some of that worship that

Einstein had for me. I wanted a guy to be a kind soul inside like Coach, a good person, someone whom I could make laugh and vice-versa. I wanted a great kisser like Sexy Lips, with the hands on the face and the sensual part of that. But lastly I was already seeing that I wanted the cherry on top. When a lucky man and I, whoever he might be, went to the bedroom (or the couch or the kitchen floor or the back seat of the car, but really how about the nice soft bed though) I wanted him to go into full on sexy time. Passionate, giving to each other, front, back, side, up down, little bites, pulling the hair, and lips everywhere.

I didn't care about jewelry or trips or fixing my car.[16] I wasn't asking for Good morning or how's your day texts.[17] He couldn't be married or living with someone but otherwise I didn't need exclusivity. I decided to K.I.S.S. Keep It Simple, Sexy. Get a drink, flirt, then go bang my brains out.

My weekend kicked off with an orgy invite from a man who is supposedly Italian, handsome, a dimple in his chin, early 40s. When I showed his bio to one of my millennial girlfriends, she said he was on her Bumble as a 33-year-old. I do not care if he is 33 or 42 or that he is lying. I am nervous (because of the squishy-in-the-middle thing) but remember I'm not supposed to worry about that now. He doesn't look 42.

He messaged me on Friday: *Do you have plans tonight?*
Cleaning? lol[18]
Later I texted: *What are you doing tonight?*
Out with a friend. You still adulting?

---

16 I might accept these though ;)

17 These are nice if they are flirty and not too intrusive.

18 Whew, I know, so sexy right? Fiyahhh

That sounded like an invitation but was it? Then this popped in: *Ok. Serious question for you. Are you open to dating boys, girls, or both?*

I read. And re-read. Am I? I don't know. I'd thought about it but wasn't sure I was ready. I texted a girlfriend to see what to do. We came up with: *Huh I haven't given it much thought. Right now I'm into guys. But I'm not ruling it out. Just not sure I'm there yet.*

Okay. Just checking. Have a couple of friends whom I team up with regularly if you might be interested.

Will definitely keep it in mind. How does that work?

Oh pretty low key. There could be full interaction, or no physical interaction, depending on how we all feel and like each other. Plenty of respect and hopefully a new friendship. :) Buongiorno!

That invite awaited, to be mulled over and considered. I was actually cleaning my loft that night, trying to be mature. I'd been invited out to a crazy night of drinking with friends but had said no because my Saturday and Sunday was filled with activities. I needed to adult, so I shopped and cleaned, but then I was sad because I was home on Friday night. I could see folks on the sidewalks going to and fro the bars while I was home scrubbing the toilet. The Audacious Bitch was telling me I was a boring person. I was tired from the week but still feeling sad and down and like a loser. I talked to Seester on the phone for two hours and felt better. That's what I needed; that connection.

I was near Hoppy's home Saturday afternoon after an all-day meeting. Less than a month ago it was our home. I had two hours to kill before a birthday celebration nearby. I called him to see if I could come lounge on the back deck, kill some time, and enjoy the sunshine. He said yes. I hadn't seen him for over two weeks. What would it be like to go to my former dream house and see him?

We sat on the deck talking about nothing important. He was closed off, but friendly. Sad, but not saying that. I kept poking at my feelings while I was there making small talk about our families and jobs. I was glad to feel really good about my decision to leave. I missed his cuddles and his companionship but I knew I'd done the right thing. Eventually he went into the house and I sat in the sun alone. He came back an hour later as I was leaving. I got three great hugs. I wonder how it felt for him. Was he hopeful I was coming back? That I would say I missed him? I find men's ability to hide their feelings quite incredible. I am incapable of it.

xoxoxo

I was supposed to get a drink with the hot Italian Orgy Man but then I realized I had double-booked myself. I had a night planned with my middle daughter. I let him go, of course. He then asked how I was coming along with my thoughts on being with a group, specifically he and another woman. I considered it. The Audacious Bitch was egging me on, "Come on now. This will be quite the adventure. You definitely should give it a go."

The common sense safe side (aka scared side) was unsure of this much intimacy with these younger people, and more than one, at this juncture in my journey. I stared at the text ten times in a half hour mulling it over. I decided if I was trying to push myself that hard it probably was not time for this type of excitement. Yet. I told him that. He said something like all things at the right time.

My middle daughter took me to Trivia Night at a local bar. We were terrible but it was fun. The man running the trivia was catching my eye the whole night, and honey, I was looking right back. He came over to talk with me at the intermission. He was very cute. Nice eyes, great smile, and I had seen some of his fun personality as he ran the trivia night.

After intermission was over, the game started back up. Audacious said to give him my number before I left. My safe side agreed this would be fine as he goes to trivia there every week and therefore was probably not a serial killer. I mean you just don't picture serial killers and trivia in the same thought do you?

I scratched my name and number on the last question slip. The daughter said it was illegible and wrote it legibly for me on the receipt. This is the daughter who didn't want me to do Bumble but she was not against me giving him my number. She said this was better because it was "an organic way to meet people." It is definitely more fun than trying to talk to people on stupid Bumble.

He came right up to me after it was over. We were being all smiley and twinkley at each other. I felt gorgeous because I got my hair done Monday night so it was still darling and curly.

After we talked for a moment about the trivia game, I made my move, whilst looking all around at everything but him and shuffling my feet in a ridiculous way, "Soooo you wouldn't be single by chance?"

He said, "Why yes I am."

I shoved my number at him, "Okay here's my number. This is the first time in my life I've ever done this."

Then I ran away. I had no thought in my head that maybe he wanted to hang out right then. I was afraid of rejection and handing him my number was all I had in me at that moment.

He texted me within a half hour that it was great to

meet me. We texted a little that evening. Trivia Man mentioned what building he lived in. It was only a few blocks from me.

When I told him, he said: *Oh my it's a party now :)*

I waited for a text from him all the next morning. I was ready for the party to start. Now. Around lunch time he asked how the day was going and we exchanged the boring chit-chat you do when you don't know someone yet.

Then he said: *We are gonna have to meet sometime for a drink at The Drum Room.*

I like this idea. I've never been there but wanted to go.

He dropped the discussion. 1 1/2 hours later I asked: *Are you more of a last minute person or a plan ahead person?*

Usually a spontaneous person. (Shocker)

I said: *That can be fun. I like both. It's fun to look forward to special things too.*

Nothinggggggggg.

I threw this at him: *My schedule blows up from this Saturday - next Friday. My only avail is tonight. Just so ya know.*

Nothinggggggggggg.

I was raring at the bit to see him that weekend. And I do love a good plan to look forward to.

At 5:52 p.m. he texted, *Afternoon.*

I waited ten whole minutes to text, *Good evening.*[19] He asked about my week. I asked about his. He mentioned the dinner he cooked. At least he wasn't dropping the ball and not texting for an hour or a day. He asked me about writing and teaching, then he called me a Renaissance woman, which I liked immensely.

Then he said: *I'm slowly starting to feel like a dip in the hot tub.*

I was hopeful he had a personal hot tub.

---

19 The games we play that are so stupid.

I said, *A dip in a hot tub is always a good idea.*

He said: *Well if I do, you are welcome to join. :)*

"IF I DO…," what kind of invitation is that? I was being so patient with this guy. I didn't think he was playing games with me. I thought maybe he was bad at texting. Possibly very busy. Maybe.

After about ten minutes I said, *When do you think you might make that decision? Lol*

I don't know. We didn't figure out your bedtime. :)

It ain't a work night. Teacher can stay out late tonight…. if she wants.

Well I got rum, whiskey, tequila and a hot tub in the basement.

Bummer, it's in the basement so it was a shared hot tub like mine.

I volleyed with, *Is that a shot glass in your pocket or are you glad to see me?*

He said, *I think it is bigger than a shot glass.*

Then *nothinggggggggggggggggg.*

I finally said, *All right I got my swimmy suit on.*

I was sitting there on my couch in a swimsuit with a sundress over it. I didn't want to start working on something else. I wanted to go bang Trivia Man this very second. What was taking so long? It had only been a few minutes but I texted, *You up for it?*

Then I said, *Don't take offense to this but you are a slowwwwwww texterrrrr and I'm being very patient with you.*

After fifteen fucking minutes he said, *Lol just give me a sec :) I am down.*

Finally after another ten minutes he said, *So do you want to walk down here?*

He better be cool.

I called Seester for a pep talk as I walked down there. I was scared out of my mind. I think it was because I had met him in real life so I had no idea of who he was.

At least on an app I could see their photos, and how they portray themselves in writing, and then through messaging I could ask some questions. Yet here I was heading to his hot tub all tra la la. Seester thought it was awesome and let's be honest, he was so cute so there was no way I wasn't going.

His building and place were gorgeous. We did a shot of whiskey at my request then we went down to the hot tub. He said it was hotter than normal and I could tell it was bothering him. We had to leave early as he was overheating. We went back upstairs. I stepped forward and kissed him. He did that super sexy thing where he pulled my jaw to go deeper in the kiss. Swooooon.

I went down on my knees to give him a BJ right there in his kitchen. He held his hand out, lifted me, and led me to the bedroom.

He said, "Let me know when you are ready for me to come."

Um what? Seriously? Gracious.

I was so turned on by the kiss in the kitchen that I came pretty quickly when he first slid into me but I didn't tap out just yet. He licked me from my throat all the way down to my toes. Then he flipped me over like I was a little trivia question slip, entering me from behind. He spanked me a couple of times just right, not too hard, not too soft. I came again but I still wanted more. He turned me back over on my back, nibbled my neck and bit my nipples. I arched into him as he pounded me with his bigger-than-a-shot-glass dick. Oh yes it was. I came a third time then panted that he could come. He did, then collapsed beside me on the bed. We lay there looking up at the ceiling. I didn't know what to say but I also kind of knew I didn't have to say anything. I had a great time but now I was ready to head back home to my own bed.

We made our way back out to the kitchen where our clothes lay in a puddle. Coital passions abated now, I did feel a bit exposed putting my swimsuit and dress back on in the middle of his kitchen, but he was getting dressed too. The damn swimsuit was wet but the dress was too short to go commando. Besides it was only three blocks.

I told him I was only interested in friends with benefits and no serious stuff. He laughed and agreed. The laugh was odd. On my walk home I tried to figure it out. Did it mean of course we were only FWBs because I was so much older than he? Or was it a sarcastic, "Of course she only wants my dick," laugh?

I hoped to make him my every Friday night activity.

This night. This sexcapade. This was what I wanted. I slept like the dead that night, fully satiated.

xoxoxo

Online dating apps began to feel like a really bad part-time job, one that I didn't get paid for and wasn't that much fun, so I deleted Bumble. The men seemed so boring, especially compared to Trivia Man. I did have some leftover Bumbles coming up. Uber Man was one of them. He wanted to meet up over the weekend, but I was busy. Even though his profile said, "Relationship," he asked what I was looking for.

Fun, flirting, a drink and see if there are sparks, maybe an FWB, I texted. *Just like my profile says.* He said he liked the FWB idea which made me wonder why he had seeking a "relationship" in his bio.[20] We texted the normal boring shit: good morning, have a good day, how was your day, what are you doing tonight, blah

---

20 Come to find out a lot of men do this. I guess they think no one will match if they put FWB.

blah blah. When he texted, *Hey sexy*, I wondered if he had forgotten my name. Is that cynical?

A few days later he messaged, *So you said something about FWB?* with a winky emoticon.

I repeated, *Yes. I believe I said: Fun, flirting, drinks, see if there's a connection. Then maybe FWB.*

What was it with this guy? What did he want? Why didn't he just ask me out?

He said, *Yes ma'am. You did. There will be.*

He was at Crossfit. He was very encouraging and detailed in answering questions about it as I'm interested, maybe, someday, in trying it. In the future ya know. After I'm fit. I don't want to die, or be the worst person in class. I said I would check it out.

He said, *When are you going to check me out?*

I replied, *You have not invited me to check you out.* He said it was implied.

We are not having a great texting convo here. I am tired of it.

I meant a time, I replied.

O when r u free, he texts. Yes he has o for oh and r for are and u for you. Hate, triple hate.

I asked if he was coming to town this weekend. He was based out of Oklahoma or something.

He said, *Is that my invite?*

To hang out? Yes. To stay at my place? No. I don't have men over to my place. It is my female sanctuary.

Oh. I guess I could sleep in my car.

I had not even met him and he wanted to crash with me for the weekend. Get a grip on reality. Did anyone fall for that bullshit? Unmatch and goodbye.

In the middle of talking to the idiotic Uber Man and hoping Trivia Man would reach out for round two, Coach texted, *I am guessing I was not selected as a possible FWB candidate?*

He was funny and a nice guy. But white old man socks and those big ass tennies and kissing like a wall. Damn it. I was not attracted. I wanted to be. A perfect FWB candidate in all the other ways, except being attracted to him, which is a definite detriment.

I said, *If it makes you feel better, no one has. How's life treating you?*

I bet my house in Vegas that you would choose a slightly aged, slightly worn out coach with loads of money in the bank... I am well if we can get the fucking school year finished.

What odds did they give you in the Vegas bet?

Negative odds, which I didn't even know was a possibility....I think they forgot I was once a finely tuned athlete. (it happens occasionally).

Hmm I always did cheer for the underdog.

That HAS to be good news for me!!!

Finely tuned athlete huh?

I am certain you were able to detect that as we enjoyed the evening, correct?

Of course.

I thought that was the case. I figured you were just too shy to say anything about it.

Can I get past old man white socks? Those come off. But that kissing. Maybe he is kinda shy and would warm up? That sense of humor is so sexy. I decided to quit thinking about it as I had no answers but something in me was saying I could easily break his heart. I wanted no entanglements, only fuck boys to match my fuck girl energy.

Trivia Man still hadn't texted by the afternoon so I said, *Just letting you know you have a great penis and you know how to use it. Much appreciated. Have a lovely day.*[21]

---

21 I should have said cock. Men like that word. Hell, I like that word. It's sexual, not an insult like "dick," and not sounding like a fifth grader saying the penis word.

Thank you! You can have it again if you want. :) tell your friends. ;)

I have told many friends of his penis but what does he mean? *Hmmm my friends aren't single but I will put up a billboard.*

Hey you never know who are swingers ;)

Why is he saying this? It's not funny. It's not flirty. It sounds like he wants to be with my friends? I. Do. Not. Understand. Play it off, *True! Will let them know!*

I enjoyed our time together but I would like some flirting and a bit of saying I'm sexy or something. I mean I was bare ass naked under him 24 hours ago. I wanted some, "I can't stop thinking about last night," or "You are so damn sexy that I'm hard right now" or "I wanna bite your nipple again," texts. I felt I deserved it after having his dick in my mouth, knees on his very clean kitchen floor. I guess I could live without that since making out with him was so hot.

I did not text him. For five whole days. The epitome of patience. I had told him I was busy for the whole next week and I was. I still wondered if we'd get to hang out again.

Thursday I texted, *Let me know if you ever want to or have time to get a drink or hang out again. ;)*

Finally heard from the dude on Friday, *We will. I just got back from a work trip.*

Ok! Great! Look forward to it. :)

So..... whennnnnnnn....[22]

xoxoxo

Since Trivia Man was being slow, I saw that I'd need to

---

22   First of all, let's repeat together, "Can you say anx-ious att-ach-ment style?" Or… maybe not, maybe just horny. I can still remember that first kiss with him. It was that pull of my jaw.

meet more men to fulfill my dreams of fun sex so I downloaded the dating app Coffee Meets Bagel. Almost immediately I was asked out. By a 60-year-old. Okay I know I'm 54, but 60? In real life if I met someone that much older, it would be nothing, but it seems like another thing on the dating app.

He didn't look that hot in his photos either. Kind of Sesame Streetish.

But this guy did things right, he asked me for drinks right off the bat. I like that, meet in person, and see if there's a connection. He texted the day before saying he was looking forward to it. He told me what he'd be wearing: blue striped dress shirt, sport coat, dress jeans. I was worried about what "dress jeans" might entail. I went all out, legs shaved, hair freshly washed, make-up, even a sexy dress. I walked into Harry's in Westport and saw him take me in like a gulp of cold water on a summer's day. The "dress" jeans looked fine.

He listened to me. He laughed at my stories. Then a half hour in, after one drink, he told me he's married to someone who doesn't care what he does. Married? What the fuck? I was so new to the apps I didn't know that many married men use the apps to cheat on their wives. Damn it to hell. I'd taken two hours to get ready. I was at least going to get some drinks and hopefully some food out of him before I left. So I let go of worrying about the whole "married" thing.

I told him my situation, that I would not be getting serious with anyone. That I'm moving in three years. We began to touch each other's hands on the table during drinks.

He said I was much prettier than my profile photos. The Audacious Bitch had decided I should kiss him when we left happy hour to go to dinner. We walked outside. I had told him I loved old buildings so he was talking about the architecture of Harry's, pointing out different things about the building. He was saying it was built in 1860 when I backed up against that old building, pulled him forward by his tie, and kissed him. When we stopped kissing, he just stood there with his eyes closed. I had no idea of the power I held in that moment. I was just bumbling through this date with my sassy dress and horniness, upending his world. I wasn't sorry though as he should have made his marital status clear before we met.

We made out on the sidewalk, in busy Westport, on a Friday night, with people flowing past. I heard someone say, "Awkward," and felt embarrassed.

We walked to dinner where the conversation was entertaining the whole time. He had been a writer in his past. Fellow writers like stories and he liked all of mine. After dinner, I asked him to walk me to my car where we made out some more before I left. He was shaking. He said thank you. He said my name like it was gold.

I thought I might see him again. He had stroked my ego with his compliments and immediate physical reaction. I felt powerful and sexy. Maybe I didn't care that he was married. That was going to be a hard and fast rule but it was more about someone cheating on someone who cared. Not someone who didn't care. Not someone so obviously in need of companionship and intimacy.[23] The reason the date went so well was that he really "got" me. He laughed at my stories, asked great questions that were thoughtful, and thought I was gorgeous. What more can you ask?

Oh yeah, maybe that they are single.

The next morning I woke up to this text from Coffee Meets Bagel (Married Guy): *I wanted to tell you these things*

---

23 Yes. I'm an idiot. Again.

while they are fresh in my mind: At Harry's your smile melted my soul. Your laugh tickled my heart. Outside the look you gave me-- that look-- stirred me deep inside. Your soft kisses-- those kisses- lit a fire deep inside of me. That fire burned again after I got home and thought about you. At dinner you showed me your mind. A strong mind in a woman is a turn on for me. At your car the world outside of us slid away, I could have stood there all night, kissing you, touching you, and holding you. Throughout the night the caress of your hand and fingers on mine was electric. I drove home on air, not land. I'm sorry if this is too much but I wanted you to know how I'm feeling. Please be patient with me if I don't always react to you in the way you might hope. I'm probably low in emotional intelligence.

Words. I'm a words girl. I keep thinking about what matters most to me. I think I crave what I haven't had maybe? Neither The Hillbilly nor Hoppy had been word guys, writing the intense poetry Married Guy had just sent.

Hoppy had provided constant cuddles, given gifts that showed he knew me, spent quality time with me, and gone above and beyond in acts of service from the minute he met me. Three months after we started dating, we went to Mexico together. I bought a special negligee for the trip, a black lacy number.[24] But when I surprised him with it, he stared at me balefully, not the reaction I was expecting. I was used to The Hillbilly who would have had the negligee off in .2 seconds. When I asked Hoppy what was going on, he said I was trying to manipulate him. I shrank inside myself in shame. I had wanted a certain reaction, a smile, a compliment, to turn him on. I didn't see how that was manipulative but maybe it was. He said those crappy words, then flipped over and fell asleep in a tequila

---

24 The very one I wore for my sex video debut on Hook-Up Dating.

haze. Unfortunately it couldn't be blamed on the tequila as it was the first of many times I would cry at not being wanted by him. I could walk through the room buck naked with nary a comment or response except perhaps derision. And yet I stayed another five years shoving sexual frustration and shame into a little box somewhere near my pancreas.

Therefore, sexual touch was at the top of my list at this moment as I was in a deficit on that. To be able to turn someone on with my physical appearance and my touch was a balm to my soul.

I texted back: *Before last night that was a rule, not to date a married man. Obviously I stayed and kissed you multiple times. I'm very attracted to your gentle spirit, your kisses and your ability to truly listen. I'm trying to decide whether to break my rule to see you. Does your wife know you go out? Does she really not care? Do you normally wear a wedding ring? I'm not sure if the first and third question matter. That's the first thing. The second is if I decide I don't care you are married, will you care that I will still date others? I'm not going to be exclusive for a long time. A long time. Like years.*

His response summarized: It's complicated with the wife, she knows he goes out but not what he does, she could check his phone but does not, he does not wear his ring. He knows I would go out with others and would be jealous but not act on it.

I called Seester for advice. She proceeded to tear me a new asshole for even thinking about having sex with a married man. Of course she was right. I texted him: *I believe at this point in time I'm gonna stick with my rule. You can know that I also felt the connection between us and that you are pretty great for me to have considered it. Thank you for telling me; it may feel as if you shouldn't have but it was right. You deserve happiness.*

He texted, *I'm sensing a struggle between your heart and*

head. I've concluded that too many times I've let the head control the heart.

I told him that I have done the opposite and let the heart control the head and that isn't good either. There has to be a balance.

A few hours later he sent this, *I can't recall a woman ever having the effect on me that you did last night. Connection? Yes, completely. This might sound desperate of me but I don't care. I respectfully ask that you give this a few days' consideration.*

I said I would but it isn't helping him as he thinks it would. It's only strengthening my resolve that I'm not breaking that rule. Not right now. Not for him. Hopefully not ever.

xoxoxo

Sexy Lips texted that he found my ring! He asked if I'd like to meet at a coffee shop to get it and I said yes. After thinking about it, I texted back and said I'd rather come over and smoke CBD with him, knowing it might lead to a hook-up. I wanted to give him another chance in the bedroom. Last time I was so nervous I couldn't relax. And everything seemed odd. And it was my first time having sex after my break up with Hoppy. My millennial girlfriends told me that the first time is always awkward and perhaps I should give Sexy Lips another chance, so I did.

He let me in and asked me if he could give me a kiss then laid a slow, sweet kiss on me. He complimented my hair and told me how beautiful my eyes were. We shared deep kisses and stared into each other's eyes.

Before we had sex, we talked about how the first time had gone and then what I wanted. I told him I'd felt very unsexy standing there naked while he was still in his boxers, that I like giving blow jobs but I wanted oral also, and that he could pull my hair and I was open to trying different things. He listened closely.

We headed upstairs. He took off his clothes while I removed mine. He kissed me, then maneuvered me to the bed, biting my nipples then moving down between my legs to tease my clit with his tongue.

He entered me, and just like last time he kept a slow rhythm. I thought, "Let's give this slow stuff a try. I mean what the hell, I'm here, you know." I purposefully made myself relax under him and go along with the ride. I was surprised to enjoy it so much that I came multiple times. I even let my voice cry out and join his moose sounds at the end.

Afterward we lay on the bed and cuddled and talked. I've been on a cuddle deficit since leaving Hoppy. I told him some stories and let myself be me. He was locked in, listening. I told him how much I liked the way he listened. He said he took the friends part of FWB seriously.

I plan to hang out with Sexy Lips once or twice a month, enjoy the sexy time, relax and talk and not have to worry about a RELATIONSHIP. That's exactly what I want.

And I got my ring back.

xoxoxo

It had been a week since Coffee Meets Bagel aka Married Guy had fallen hard to my wiles. I was glowing the night we went out. I felt gorgeous and empowered and amazing. How was I to know he'd been in a loveless marriage for years and hadn't had sex in 18 months?

I got a text from him, *I've been holding my fingers away from the keyboard but can't anymore. I think I have your heart. I need to convince your head. Nobody likes side drama. I'm guessing that's part of your concern. Yesterday I thought about what it would be like not to see you again. I cried a little. I haven't cried over a girl since I was 18. I know that sounds weak of me but that's how I feel about you. I want to see your wild side. I want to wander with you at least a little.*

Respectfully, CMB

I texted back, *I am following my head. You are correct. The reason I am doing that is that following my heart only has gotten me two long-term relationships that weren't what I needed. I'm going with the head first now and then only tiny bits of the heart are allowed to engage. I'm dedicated to doing that for the next three years.*

That's what I need right now. And what I will do.

I do not want you to leave your wife for me as I am in no place for a relationship with anyone. I don't want anyone to expect my texts, my time, my kisses.[25]

I think you should leave your wife for yourself. You have a lot of life in you. Why waste a day? I left a 28-year-marriage with a 13-year-old son to parent on my own because life is too short to live with people you don't love.

I know you are a decent person and I very much enjoyed our time together. Perhaps I should have left immediately when you told me. I am sorry if that caused you pain.

Courage dear-heart. Think about what you need in life and go for the gusto. So many don't have the choice to live life to the fullest. We do. The head wins.

He texted and said he understood and that if we didn't learn from our experiences we'd be fools. He gave all the reasons why he couldn't leave his wife, even though I was not asking him to leave. I stated that his excuses were moot points, that people leave in much worse circumstances than his. Mine for example.

Then he said, *Since Sunday, I've been on an emotional high.*

---

25 Wow, I sound badass. Where did this woman go? Oh yeah... I wasn't in love.

56

I've treated everybody in a kinder, gentler way. I used to think that love at first sight did not exist. After you first walked into Harry's, our eyes locked. Our hands touched. For about three seconds I could not move or think. I saw a woman who was beautiful, was searching for something and liked what she saw in me. Our remaining time solidified the first three seconds.

Yes, my heart is broken. I'm crying a little as I write this. I'm used to being the heartbreaker, not the heartbroken. Of course, pain goes with living. It is the reason that I will have that pain that will haunt me.

Know that I have a piece of your heart. I know you have a piece of mine. You had me at soft kisses. This is crazy, I know, but I must say it. **I love you.**

Whoaaaaaa. The L-word. I'm sorry if it's mean but I felt super empowered by this. He'd been in a downward spiral of life, a loveless marriage, trapped. He'd said his last relationship was a younger woman who wanted his money. How long had it been since someone had treated him special? Years I'm betting. I listened to him, asked questions, told him stories of myself, and my writing. I kissed him. I initiated it. I don't feel bad about it. I wanted to and I did. We are grown-ass adults. And of course it wasn't "love," it was lust, but love sounds so much nicer.

I'm still not gonna see him though. Onward and upward.

xoxoxo

Tantric Man's profile stated that he was into tantra and that he doesn't have much time so don't expect that, he doesn't want a relationship, and just wants to enjoy. Perfect. It took a few weeks to schedule but finally we set a meet-up at Parlor in the Crossroads. It's like a fancy adult food court with two bars and six restaurants in it.

I walked in to find him already at the bar, a six foot tall athletic golden boy, just like his photos. He immediately began rubbing his hand on my back. I was very attracted to him even though he seemed a bit arrogant. We talked about our lives.

He was a very intense listener, repeating back to me what I said with a question, kind of like a therapist does. He also claimed to really know people. He wants a second date with me so perhaps he does. He liked that I write, my energy, and my positive outlook on life, that I'm open to experiencing new things.

He actually told me that when he meets people he is trying to find reasons to say no to hanging out with them again, to mark them off as a possibility. He said he didn't find any with me. It felt a tiny bit like a job interview, one I have decided I want as I think it will pay in some luscious benefits for me.

Then he saw a woman he knew. She came over and I really liked her. He said these were the kind of healthy, positive people he hung out with and I think I would like to meet some of his friends. He has a woman friend who is into him and also into women so if/when I want I can give that a go. [26]

Tantric Man is a go. We will meet for a midday break in two weeks.

In other news, Trivia Man has been incommunicado. He said he wanted to hang out again. Since he said he liked spontaneity I challenged him this morning to hang out sometime between noon and nine

---

[26] This turned out to be a damn wife but I wouldn't know that for months.

with me. Did not even get a text back. Damn it. [27]

Things are pretty great. I love living by myself and actually can't believe I get to do this. All women need to know how awesome it is to live by yourself. Do it.

---

[27] Trivia Man and I never hung out again. I did see him several years later when a lover and I went to play trivia though. I think he recognized me ;).

Normal programming has been suspended

Summer 2019

Memorial Day Weekend

I decided to try out the Hinge dating app since Bumble was so boring. My first match had photos that included a close up of his face, (short white hair, smile lines, sparkling blue eyes and a great smile); a photo on the beach with his daughter, (arm loosely around her shoulders); and a photo at the pool relaxing on a lounge chair, (tan lanky body, knobby knees crossed).

He was flirty and funny and asked me for a drink, saying I could choose the place. I chose Afterword Tavern, a combination bar/bookstore with a killer old-fashioned, down in the Crossroads Arts District. I set out that afternoon to walk the mile there. I was in a great mood as the sun wrapped me in its golden warmth and summer stretched before me full of possibilities. I was wearing a red dress that showed off my legs. As I walked past The Midland Theater, I saw people lined up outside awaiting a concert. It was a favorite activity of mine to try and guess who was playing based on the crowd waiting to get in. The fans were in full black emo-esque regalia.

I asked a young woman in a skull t-shirt who was playing.

"In This Moment," she replied.

I couldn't believe it. They were my favorite metal band, one of the few metal bands I liked. I decided I'd go meet Hinge #1 for an hour then I'd walk back to my place, change into jeans and a requisite black t-shirt and go to the concert. I mulled this at a busy intersection as I waited to cross.

"Ma'am?" A man in a pickup truck waiting for the light smiled and blew a kiss at me then said, "Beautiful. Thank you."

I smiled, the light turned green, he rolled up his window and drove away. My walk had an extra swing to it those last few blocks. I felt beautiful as I walked in Afterword. Hinge jumped up from the couch he was waiting on, we leaned in for a quick hug, then he told me to tell the bartender to put my drink on his tab. I wasn't going to do that. I wanted him to buy my drink but I didn't want to have to say it to the bartender so I dawdled then decided to buy my own damn drink. Hinge saw something was up and hustled his ass over to tell the bartender himself, making a better second impression than the first. We talked and laughed and drank. I told him I was going to a concert after this and that he could come if he'd like.

"Sure! Let's go!" he said.

"You don't even know who's playing," I said.

"Who cares! I'm in!"

I re-assessed him. He looked old but maybe he didn't act old. He drove us closer to my place, came in while I changed, then we walked a block away to grab a slice of pizza at Milwaukee Deli, a favorite of mine.

"We are on a date now right?" he asked.

I raised my eyebrows. "A date?"

"Yes, we had the meetup and now this is a date," he said.

"Sure I guess so," I laughed.

"What are you doing tomorrow?" he asked.

"Riding my bike ten miles and maybe kayaking," I said.

"I haven't ridden in years but I could get my bike out and go with you," he offered.

"Nah, I'd leave you in the dust," I teased. I liked biking alone. It was a sort of meditation that eased the constant flow of thoughts.

"You definitely would!" he agreed. "I'd come paddle with you after if you'd like."

I said I'd think about it. I liked that he liked me but I also liked doing some things alone.

The forecasted thunder storm arrived, skies opened up flooding the streets. He impressed me by ordering an Uber to take us the four blocks to the concert.

We got whiskey drinks in plastic cups and stood at the back of the crowd in front of the stage. The band came on. I danced and screamed just like I'd have done alone. He watched me, smiling. He kissed me after a few songs, then the alcohol and music fueled a make out session right there amidst the mosh pit and laser lights. At one point I worried what the people near us thought but they seemed to be focused on the stage so I closed my eyes and enjoyed his mouth on mine, tongues engaged in play. After the concert he held my flimsy travel umbrella over us as we walked back to my place through the gentle rain. As we turned a corner, the wind swooshed between buildings flipping the umbrella up, snapping it. We looked at each other with wide eyes, then clutched each other in laughter before tossing the umbrella in the trash can, holding hands to run the last two blocks.

We made out in the elevator but when we stepped in my door I stepped back. I didn't want to sleep with him that night. This already felt like more than a hookup.

"You better get some sleep for your bike ride," he said.

"Yes, I should," I agreed. He gave me a quick kiss and walked out saying he'd text the next day.

I biked eleven miles the next morning then headed to his place as he'd invited me to hang out at his apartment pool. He lived in one of those complexes that have twenty buildings that all look alike. I drove past the pool twice before calling him to say I was lost. He came down and stood in the parking lot and talked me to where he was. We walked up the stairs, he opened his door, and gave me a quick tour. I was pleased to see a full bookshelf and a shelf of cool finds from the ocean, some of which he'd found scuba diving. We hadn't kissed except a peck when I'd arrived, both a bit shy now, sober in the daylight. He showed me the bathroom where I changed into my swimsuit. I stepped out into the hall. He was standing there in his swimming trunks. He took me in his arms and kissed me. I closed the gap between us, heated, wanting him. The swimsuits came off quickly, lips staying engaged throughout.

We collapsed together on his bed a few feet away. His mouth was kissing my throat then teasing and biting my nipples. I arched up moaning. He slid into me, filling me, the movement hit my G-spot immediately. I exploded, coming all over both of us. Our bodies took over. The sex was fast and physical. I came again, then he came. In fifteen minutes we'd progressed from looking at some seashells to the hottest sex I'd ever had. We lay there on our backs, breathing hard, looking at each other. I was smiling at him. He was not smiling. His eyes were wide open in wonder, looking at me like I was an alien.

"What was that?" he asked.

I shrugged as I didn't know what to say. "It was amazing," I said.

"Amazing? That was…" he struggled. "It was… It's never felt like that before. You are so goddamn beautiful." He shook his head.

The sex and the words were an elixir. I drank them. I'd been starving for this. We had sex again before we stumbled out to the pool.

I stayed the night. Then the next night. We'd clocked in at eight times in 48 hours when I prepared to go home on Memorial Day.

"Hold on," he said, digging through a drawer, then he handed me a key. "Go ahead and put this on your keychain. It's yours."

I looked down at the key in my palm, trying to understand, then the realized he was giving me a key to his place after knowing me for one weekend.[28] It had taken Hoppy two years to give me a key to his place. That was too long but this seemed way too fast.

"I don't want a key to your place," I said, handing it back.

"It's a lot easier for me," he said. "You'll be able to let yourself in downstairs."

I put it on my keychain.

In the first week with Hinge #1 I was fucked properly for the first time in my life. Up, down, sideways and front-ways. I was told I was beautiful with

---

[28] Can you say "love-bombing"?

reverence. I saw a dad who loved his daughter so much that he literally cried when I played him the Michael Buble' song, *Forever Now*. He wrote a five couplet poem for me, played my music on the speaker, and opened every door for me. He has made me laugh. He knew I was smart and that I would call him on his bullshit. And is okay with that. He seemed to think I was the most beautiful creature who's ever existed.

In six days, he wrote and spoke the words I've needed to hear the last six years.

He liked who I was. So far.

I think he's smart for liking who I am.

I think I'm not ready for him. He could be someone I could spend my life with. Just sayin'. It's possible.[29]

xoxoxo

Fourth of July

Hinge and I had been boning and sunning for four weeks. We'd even said I love you. He cooked for me, we smoked cigars together on his deck. I had agreed to be exclusive after he'd bugged me about it for two weeks. I didn't like the idea of monogamy so soon again but I did like him and I didn't need sex from anyone else as we were having sex two or three times a day. Good sex. Really really good sex. We joked about how we could make old people porn, and it would sell.

My sisters, their men, and their kids were getting together at my parent's farm in the Ozarks to celebrate the Fourth as usual. He wanted to go, badly, so after running it by my parents I invited him. We sat around in lawn chairs, iced tea in hand, talking. Hinge lapped up my dad's riches to rags to riches stories. After hot

---

[29] Ergo the monogamy problem rears its ugly head.

dogs and chips, we watched the few fireworks someone had brought. We were picking up the dregs of fireworks when Hinge stood up from his lawn chair and held his phone in the air playing the Star-Spangled Banner. I looked at Seester and rolled my eyes at this ridiculousness. She looked at him and smirked.

"I hope you don't expect me to put my hand on my heart," Seester said.

"As long as you don't kneel," he sneered, referring to the Colin Kapernick protest.

"I'll fucking kneel if I want to," she shot back.

He shut up.

An hour later we were in my childhood bedroom. He brought it up and we ended up talking for a solid hour about civil rights and freedom. He said he saw a different perspective and thanked me then we had sex, quiet like mice, as my parents were sleeping in the next room.

xoxoxo

Labor Day

"You've given me some advice recently to help my life, so now I'm going to give you some," he said. Surprised at the snarkiness emanating from him, I stopped putting away the groceries, interested to see what he had to say. He stood with the ramrod straight posture he'd kept from his military years beside my bright purple barstool behind the bar that separated the kitchen from the living room.

"Your bathtub is disgusting," he pointed a finger at me. "You should have cleaned that before they came over."

My sister and niece had stayed in my apartment on their visit to Kansas City over the Labor Day weekend.

I'd stayed with him, as I did every weekend, but he was in my place now since I had school the next day.

"My sister doesn't give a shit about my tub," I said.

"I don't care if it was family. You should have cleaned it better," he said.

I remembered that I'd been in a huge rush Friday before they came as he'd wanted me at his place at a certain time, cutting short my cleaning but I knew this would not suffice. In his mind it should always be immaculate. Also what the fuck was he going on about me giving him advice? I'd encouraged him in his job hunting that weekend, was that it? He hadn't worked in a year and a half. He had been living off a big severance just hanging out at the damn pool and watching TV.

"Look, my life is never going to revolve around cleaning my bathtub. I just don't care. Also, it isn't even that bad," I responded.

His eyes were red and owly, "If you'd let me have a key I could have cleaned it for you." He'd been asking me for a key the last few weeks. I'd dodged it. I didn't know why I didn't want to give him one; we'd been dating for two months. He'd given me a key to his place on our first weekend together. At that time I thought it was romantic. Later I realized he didn't like getting up to let me in. Now he wanted one to my place. The week before as we were walking to his car to do some errands he said we had time to go to the hardware store and get a key made.

"I don't want to do that," I heard myself say. He stopped walking, keys dangling from his hand, to look at me. The sun scorched the top of my head while heat rose off the black asphalt baking my feet through flimsy sandals. The hot wet air blanketed my body, holding me down. His shock mirrored mine. I didn't know I was going to say it. It had come from deep inside, a resounding fuck no. I just knew it was true, which is what I told him when we got in the car and he turned to ask why. I told him that he began dating a not-quite-formed person, one who is figuring out who she is. One who is not ready for a lifetime commitment. He seemed to think saying I love you means a commitment. I told him that it's like the Mother May I game. In three steps he's at the end of the line and I'm still taking baby steps to get there. He interrupted to say that there are still steps, living together and maybe getting married. Can you love who someone is, but not really want to commit to them fully?

I'm listening to that inner voice that said no to the key to my place and I'm backing off. A key is an honor, a symbol of trust. He wanted to enter my world whenever he wished. I wanted to retain my right to keep him, and anyone else, out. We started dating one fucking month after I left Hoppy Sporty Sport. I was not looking for a relationship, just another fuckboy to add to the stable. Well I definitely got a fuckboy but I also got someone who's crazy in love with me. I wondered if something is wrong with me because he was wonderful in so many ways. Damn it, the sex with him was crazy good.

The next week we decided that I should spend some time alone so instead of staying at his place the whole weekend I came home Saturday morning.

I was alone for 28 straight hours. It was peaceful.

A little unnerving.

Uncomfortable at times.

I leaned into it.

I wasn't trying to please anyone else. I didn't have to compromise on writing and reading and napping and getting some work done. It was pretty fucking wonderful. A bit lonely. I went on a nine-mile bike ride, ate a delicious salad, took a two-hour nap, made chicken and salad for dinner, did homework for my college classes, and went to bed at midnight. I got up when I wanted, without someone saying that I "slept half the day away." I made a fuckton of bacon and eggs and feasted on it, watched a movie on Netflix, ran to the corner store in the rain for coffee creamer without someone shaking their head at my lack of planning. No one was upset that I don't have local TV and they couldn't watch the news at 6:30 a.m. I was getting ready to go out and felt fucking tired so I took a one hour nap. I walked down to Milwaukee Deli and had a Cubano and a pear cider and read *Women Who Run With The Wolves*. I'm getting back to my Wild Woman self. I realized I'd gotten in too deep with Hinge. He wanted to get serious and I just wasn't ready.

After two full days of solitude, I went to Hinge's house Monday night for dinner and sex. We left the key discussion alone and just kept things chill. Tuesday night I was working on some homework but images of Hinge kept popping in my head. They were all in bed. These were our best times. Whether it was rollicking, frollicking goddamn great sex or me with my head on his shoulder listening to him talk about the great things he sees in me.[30]

My head keeps trying to get me to rethink this break-up. Wednesday night he was being a bossy pants about some reunion thing Friday that he wanted me to go to. I told him I needed some space to think for a bit. But I know. I know it's over. My heart isn't in it.

Head: yes. Heart: No. They both need to be a yes.

---

30 That ego gets you in trouble every single time beeshes.

WTF heart. What's your deal?[31] I gotta listen to it. I know it's right. Damnit. Let the broken begin so the healing can happen.

Saturday morning I texted to ask if I could drop by his place after my bike ride. It had been a few days since I'd asked for time to think. He asked what time. I said I would let him know and if he was busy I'd come back later. He said, "Not busy. Just might go to the pool." I think he specifically said this to see if I'd say I wanted to go with him to the pool. If I didn't say that, he knew I was coming to break up.

I texted back after the ride and he said to come over. I started crying when I was a mile away. I cried all the way in, using the key he'd given me 48 hours after we met. I walked up the stairs, crying. I stopped to look through the window on the landing at the ducks by the pond for the last time. I stood by the door for the last time. I knocked. He said to come in. Of course he didn't get up. As usual. He was in his recliner two feet from the door.

I walked in crying. He was sitting there in my favorite pair of shorts of his, the blue ones with fish skeletons.[32] He had his glasses on so he was sort of Anderson-Cooperish looking... if you squint. He was holding a pen, pretending to work on a Sudoku.

I set the bag of his things I'd collected from my place gently on the counter in the kitchen and came back into the small living room.

"Is that my stuff?" he asked.

I nodded and sat down in the chair that I hated and would never sit in again, one of those things with two

---

31 It saw past the ego stuff and knew we were not compatible.

32 He wore these on our first date and knew I liked them. Props to him for pulling out all the stops though.

recliners and a place to keep things in the middle, so you can't lay down and you can't cuddle at all.

"I've got yours ready. I figured that's why you were here," he said, getting up.

He set it by the door and walked over. He didn't sit back down.

"I'd like that $60 if you've got it," he said.

He'd bought something or other that I said I would pay him for. I couldn't believe he'd ask for it. I'd already thought of it but what a dick to bring it up. I told him it was in the bag with the clothes. He nodded. I'm was waiting for him to sit down so we could talk.

"Well I won't keep you. I know you have places to go," he said, still standing.

I looked up at him through my tears, "Ok."

I grabbed the bag full of my clothes and books and make-up items that I'd been dragging in all summer because I was that serious about him.

He opened the door. I walked out. He watched me. My tears were falling but I held the sobs in. He watched me walk down the stairs.

"I'll talk to you later," he said.

No, you won't, I thought as the sobs overtook me at the car.

I cried part of the way driving home but started feeling better pretty quickly. He'd been such a dick, "Where's my sixty bucks?" and "I'm sure you have places to go." I thought about how I'd been just beginning my slut journey back in May and how he'd slipped past my No-Relationship, Only-Fun gatekeepers.

#1 I thought cute pineapple shirt meant out of the box.

He wore a cute mint green pineapple shirt on our first

date which made me think he was different. He never wore that shirt again. I wonder why?

He was very in the box. That's not what I want.

In the box as in his normal gear is golf wear not pineapple shirts.

In the box as in his favorite Friday night activity was to grill and watch *America's Got Talent*.

In the box as in telling me he didn't like the idea of my planned half-sleeve tattoo, that I didn't need it to be "beautiful." (I told him the first weekend and he thought it was fine; he brought it up weeks later.)

In the box as in living in the whitest, most chain store/restaurant area in the metro area.

In the box as in not taking adventures on his own.

As in he worried about a little PDA if we were in his hood but not other places, like when he came to school and leaned over and kissed me in the hall. Granted there were no students there but an admin could have seen it. That's not in the box; that's just asshole.

#2 He talked the talk.

I'd never been with a dude who could communicate. I was enamored. I'd lay my head on his chest post-coitus and he'd tell me how fucking awesome and gorgeous and amazing I was. Who doesn't like that?

Outside of the bedroom however he was so fatherly with communication. I was scolded for putting the spoon I'd just stirred my coffee with back on the counter. I was told my car was disgusting. I learned that you must wash the dishes fully before putting them in the dishwasher.

He gives me shit about stuff that is dumb. He'll say how I don't cook for him. Nope. I haven't very much. So what? I know he's just joking but some people joke like that to get their point across in a sneaky way. Also it just ain't funny. It's passive aggressive.

Other fatherly talking was just telling me too many details about boring shit. He always wanted to teach me something. 95% of the time I already knew it. 3% of the time it was interesting. 2% of the time I didn't know it and didn't care.

#3 He was too much THE MAN.

He thought he was learned because he watched both Fox News and CNN. I stopped trying to talk politics with him because he'd jump all over what I was trying to say. I don't wish to debate. I wish to converse and listen and learn, which we'd get around to, sometimes, if I had enough patience.

He watched too much TV, was on Facebook too much, but thought he was knowledgeable about stuff. On a related note, he doesn't read. I thought he was a reader when I first met him because he has a bookshelf with books. I gave him three books for his birthday. He read none of them. One was even a goddamn Kama Sutra book and we never used it once.

He said too many things that were so fucked, from racist jokes to homophobic jokes. These came out in the last month or so. Early on it was stupid Facebook memes. He went to a drag Bingo with me in our first two weeks. When he put a five dollar bill in his mouth for the queen to take, I thought he was cool. He's not.

#4 He was cranky.

He'd call his rental office to complain about the carpet not being vacuumed in the hallway. Whatever. But then I had to hear about it.

One day there weren't baskets at the grocery store, the little carry baskets, and he lost his shit. He found a manager because it had happened several times before.

I understand you need to get your groceries but you don't yell at someone about it. And there are carts…

He was constantly complaining and they were first world problems, all of them. I am officially renaming him Cranky Pants. It's actually funny I never gave him an actual name, just Hinge #1, for the damn dating app. So telling?

#5 Bleh. There's more but I'm not feeling it.
Thing is he was great too. And that's why I stayed. He encouraged me, helped me, cooked for me, helped with shit I had to do, sometimes he listened to me. He thought I was smart and beautiful and amazing. The sex was off the charts.

Looking ahead.

Did a bat signal go out?

She's singggggllle...

September 2019

In a very strange manner of events, three men circled into my universe the very day I broke up with Cranky Pants. I was looking out my loft window, writing, as I do, a la Sex in the City style. I thought I saw Sexy Lips walk past. He was looking fine, in a suit. I texted him, *Did you just walk past my window?"*

Why yes I did, he texted an hour later. *I was at a wedding.*

We talked about seeing each other again sometime. I'd only been single a few hours and a man with whom I could probably set up a sexcapade in one text walked past. I don't know if I want to see him again, but still.

Then Coffee Meets Bagel/Used to Be Married Guy texted, telling me that David Sedaris, a favorite author of mine, (that I mentioned on our ONE date where Coffee FELL IN LOVE with me), was coming to town.

He said I should get a ticket. He said he'd be there. I'm wondering if he has a calendar suggestion set to check on me every six weeks. I didn't respond. I'm not looking backward.

Except for one…

Out of the blue Tantric Man texted me when I was headed to Cranky's place to break up.

We are having dinner next week.

xoxoxo

Remember when I downloaded the HUD app back in April the first weekend I was single after Hoppy Sporty-Sport? I did the same thing now that I'm single again. Back in the saddle again. Completely different experience this time.

He looked fairly normal on his pix, meaning he was looking into the camera and actually smiling and had clothes on. I asked if he was married in my response to his first message. Negative. I noted that I was "1,000 years older." He said he was attracted to me so it didn't matter.

I messaged: *Curious what you'd like to come out of this honestly. What would be the best thing you could think of tonight?*

Have a good time with good company and if we end up making out at the end of the night that's a bonus. How about you?

I agreed and said I was looking for nothing serious and that I just broke up with someone. That I was just looking for flirting and fun. He liked this. He asked me to meet this weekend. I mentioned a time in a few hours at John's Big Deck. He agreed. Then my stomach started hurting.

Looking back at his profile later, I could see he didn't post a completely current picture. He had a very long beard, but it was a nice-looking one. He was bigger in

76

real life. We talked and it felt really awkward. I asked what it was like to date at his age (34), if he was looking for a serious relationship, (not me, of course), but otherwise. He explained that he was and that it was really hard because it was mostly single moms on dating apps. He had no problem with someone having kids. He said it was hard to start a relationship when they could only go on dates about once every two weeks. I told him some funny dating stories. He laughed his ass off. We talked for a couple of hours.

He put his hand on my leg and then my back and then my butt. It was nice.

We kissed.

We left the bar and came to a bench near my place and full-on made out. I may have been sitting on top of him on that bench.

I decided he needed to come on up.

Then it was not great.

He was super nice and a great kisser but I believe he almost had a heart attack about ten minutes into the sexual relations. He had to stop and ask for a glass of water.

Insert eyebrow wiggle. I was a bit much for him I guess.

I took over on top but it just wasn't awesome. Then the best part was he did some stuff with his hands. It was nowhere near as amazing, like-not-even-close to what it was with Cranky. Ughhhh. Please God I can have that sex again in my life? Pleeeeeaaaasssse.

I don't want to miss Cranky. He was kind of adorable. Also not adorable at all. Let's remember that moment when he was looking at me with owly red eyes and explaining how I wasn't good enough because my tub wasn't immaculate. Fuck. That. Shit.

Sigh.

Ok let me finish with HUD #2. First of all he didn't finish. I tried really hard but no go.

He said, "So how does the overnight parking work down here?"

Oh no.

I didn't want him to stay. I said I didn't know. Then I said I had a 12-mile bike ride in the morning so I had to get up really early. He took the hint and left.

Next time I will make this clear before anyone comes in. No overnights.

Hey I bagged someone 20 years younger. Not a hottie but a super nice guy who was fun to talk to and make-out with. On to bigger and better things. I hope.

xoxoxo

I did the dumbest thing. I looked at all of the couple photos of Hoppy and me on Facebook, all six years of them. Goofy tequila smiles, arms loose over each other's shoulders, his Blues hat sideways on my head. Frosting dabbed on each other's noses while decorating cookies. And my favorite of all, in Christmas sweaters by the huge tree in Union Station, his hand on my waist leaning forward looking into my eyes saying something funny. I'm laughing and looking right back, so in love.

Of course I didn't post the hard moments. I walked down memory lane and thought I would be fine, that I could handle it.

But then I played Adele while I was making dinner. And I was tired and I was hungry. I cried a little. I missed his hugs and sweet kisses.

I did the right thing. I took a nap and ate. I went for a run outside in the sunshine in my beautiful city and I felt kick-ass cool. During my run I thought about what I wanted:

1. **Friends-with-benefits.** Someone to have a drink with or go listen to music, to laugh and talk and flirt and have sex with. But not text everyday, not even see each other every week.

2. **Independence.** I don't want to plan my life around anyone except myself right now. No, "Why are you staying up so late?" Or "Why are you on the phone so long?" Or "I don't want to eat that." None of that.

3. **Fun.** I don't mind at all riding my bike by myself, running, working out, going to a gallery, shop, reading, or watching a film. I'm still working up to the idea that I could go to a concert alone, and happy hour.

4. **Light sexy banter.** I want to flirt and be flirted with.

xoxoxo

I was waiting at a stoplight at the Whole Foods in South Plaza, heading to the bike trail so my bike was on the rack of my car. My dream man went whizzing by me on his own bicycle. Oh. My. God.

He was on a road bike, no helmet so I don't think he rode very far. He had a messenger bag slung over his shoulder resting on his back. His hair was black and curled on his collar. It had little flecks of gray in it. He is in his 40s or 50s and fucking hot. Yes I was able to ascertain this as he rode past. I was stopped at a light, remember? And I was gawking.

I must have him. I will be hanging out at this intersection again soon. At 11 on a Saturday. To see. You know. If he goes by again.

I'm not ready for him. I have a lot of growing to do. But I saw him.

After I saw my future man, I rode my bike 8+ miles and wanted a burger. I was near the home where I lived with Hoppy for two years so I thought what the hell and asked if he'd like to meet me. He was heading out to do the same thing in fifteen minutes, so we met at a little bar. We were always good friends, good companions. He jumped right in, talking about work for 10 minutes straight then asked about my work. We talked about family. He made me laugh several times. We hugged, platonic, very platonic. It was good. I didn't want to kiss him or anything like that. I said maybe we could be friends now and he said it depends or something. He was always great at the non-answer.

Today, I deleted Cranky Pants' number. All of his pictures on my phone, fully deleted. Except one. I kept one for posterity.

He wasn't cute at all. Well, he grew on me. He had a great penis. But he was a pain in the ass and I'm already glad I don't have to make plans with him. I've got to pay more attention to my own wisdom. Stop trying to give people so many chances. These men don't show their true colors until two or three months in. Sit back and just see what they are. The first few months they are chameleons. That's what.

xoxoxo

I went back to Bumble and matched with a long lean cyclist. He was the youngest person I'd matched with at 33 years old, 21 years younger than me.[33]

His profile had two truths and a lie: "I like the outdoors, I'm kinky and a conservative."

I ventured a guess: "I'm thinking the lie is that you're

---

[33] This was older than my oldest child, by a few years, in case you were wondering.

conservative."

"You are very right. Hopefully that means you dig the other two."

I said it depended on what kinky meant to him. He said it could mean many things. We chitted and chatted and decided to meet. On a Wednesday. He invited me to his hotel room which was 25 minutes away so I invited him to my place with some rules:

Meet for a drink first.

My bedtime was 9.

By myself.

He agreed. He asked what I'd be wearing and I went with the red dress I wore on first date with Cranky Pants. He said not to wear any underwear. I obeyed.

We met at Dott Boss, a cute bar with way too many lights, a block away from my place. I saw him come in and watched as he went up to another woman in a red dress and introduced himself. He hadn't seen me because I was behind the bar, which embarrassed the hell out of him and made me laugh. He sat on the bar stool next to me. He didn't want his own drink so we shared my Old-Fashioned and made small talk. He asked if I felt ready.

I was.

We walked to my place. The minute the elevator door shut he had me against the wall giving me a deep kiss. We parted to walk to my door. I fumbled getting the key in. Before the door was fully shut behind us he had my dress up already going at it with his tongue. Lordy be. I could barely stand. We threw our clothes off and fell on the bed. He needed to back off a tiny bit on his hand pressure in the clitoral region, but other than that. Hell yes, hell yes.

It was the best booty call I've ever had. (Okay, it wasn't as good as Cranky Pants. However, it was the first time so there's a handicap, like in golf.)

It was rough and tumble, not too rough. Just enough tumble.

Afterward we lounged naked and talked about former relationships. I told him I was meeting Tantric Man the next day. He gave me some tips on hanging out with people in open relationships. He realized he needed to go as it was past 8:30. He told me to message him my number in the app.

He put his jeans on, sans underwear, which he'd used to wipe me down after coming on my stomach. Then he stuffed the underwear down his jeans to walk out. I realized later it probably would have been good form to offer him a plastic bag or perhaps a glass of water.

xoxoxo

It was finally time to meet Tantric Man. We'd had a first meetup way back in May just before I got exclusive with Cranky but never had a real "date." We met at Brown & Loe, a home-owned restaurant with great locally-sourced food, and talked for an hour about our lives, our summers, work and family. He's a little full of himself but he's fit, smart, and has a hot car so no wonder. I don't mind a little arrogance since I'm not gonna be with this guy forever, just an FWB situation.

We headed to my place after dinner. I played show and tell with all the cool shit I have at my place, my antique typewriters and old cameras and such. He was nice and admired everything.

We began kissing on the couch. I reminded myself to slow down. And then slow down more. And then even more. We moved to the bed. It was the slowest thing I've ever done.

I got into my yoga brain during sex. It was so

different from anything I've done. I had to keep telling myself to calm down. To relax and enjoy. I got on top first. We breathed together. He was shaking a little bit. Then he did this great position where he wrapped his leg around mine and was on my side. I don't even know. We didn't know how to stop. We were an hour in and just had to decide to stop. Finally a true FWB. We set two dates for the next month.

xoxoxo

I started grad school classes in the summer to get a counseling degree for when I retire from teaching. I walked into my first class, ten minutes early of course. There was already a young man sitting at the long table, mid-20s, sparkling blue eyes, a bit of a pompadour sticking up. He had his binder, pen, notebook, computer, and phone all laid out in a perfect perpendicular fashion in front of him.

"What the fuck with 125 pages of reading before the first class?" I asked him.

His eyebrows shot up. He smiled but didn't say anything. I thought, well he will never speak to me again.

The young man and I didn't know anyone so we ended up sitting by each other often, not talking much, just a known entity. When I saw that one of the classes we needed was only offered on the main campus, over an hour away. I gingerly asked him if he'd like to ride together. At his ecstatic yes, we figured out he loves to drive, and I hate it. On our first ride there we talked non-stop about school since we were both teachers. On the way home, he was playing Lizzo and an impromptu singalong dance party broke out in the car. I've learned so much about the gay world while he's learned some about my female experience. We went out on the town for the first time this week. After our second tequila shot, I was telling him about Tantric Man. He asked to see my Tinder, was askance that I'd never had one so we set it up right then, then we sat there and swiped on people. We laughed and drank and danced. My head hurts a little from all the tequila but my heart is full. He would become my best Boo.

A Slut is Born

October 2019

Is it "okay" who I want to be, at least who I want to be right now? When I reveal who I am right now to people it is shocking to many of them. Is it because I'm in the Bible belt of the U.S.?

Who am I right now? I am a woman who doesn't want a full-time man, doesn't want one man completely BUT does want to date and have sex with many men. How dare I? Why do I think I can break the system?

I'm not following the norm of one-man one-woman but I'm also not following the feminist idea of not needing men.

I was at the homestead with my parents a few weeks ago. My father told me I'd be a white-haired lonely cat lady with saggy boobs because I've broken up with all three of my relationships. I think he was trying to be funny.

He wasn't.

What was funny was my mom saying very quietly

under her breath, "She'll be happy."

Not even an hour later when I told my mom I was "texting menz" to be funny and just share a bit of my life with her she said, "Why do you need a man? Can't you just be alone for a while?"

That was the message I got (except from my inner circle). It's not okay what I want. I should either want one man or none. You can't have a bunch.

Why not?

When they hear I'm dating lots of men, most people look at me with distrust for one of two reasons, which cracks me up because they are opposite sides of the camp.

Heretical belief #1: I don't have a man nor want one steady person.

"Oh you'll want one man. You just haven't found the right guy," they say. They look at me with a side-eyed glance of judgment.

I mean, why would you not want a man telling you what's good about you and what's not good? Why would you not want to eat when you want, sleep when you want, clean your goddamn bathtub when you want, put the sheets on the bed how you want and pay your bills how you want? These are some of the things my exes wanted and I gave it to them because really who cares?

I guess I do. I like doing all these things how I want. I like writing at 5 a.m. and no one is bothered or bothering me.

I'm not looking for Mr. Right nor do I want to meet him right now. I do want to find him in a few years. I think.

Maybe not?

Maybe can I just do this whole slut thing for the rest

of my life?

I mean.

Maybe.

Heretical belief #2: I want to date lots of men and not be exclusive.

Just be alone already. Why can't you? Are you not strong enough? Why are you on dating sites? Just make some girlfriends and have some fun. This is the kickback I get from some women.

"Oh I don't even want a man. I like my life the way it is." Me too honey, but I like dick. I like men. I like flirting. I like meeting new people. So I'm straddling these two worlds of one-man one-woman and just be on your own feminism with my own brand of feminism. I am deeming it my year of sluttery. I'm dating and having lots of sex. I'm forthright with everyone I date about all of it. I'm dedicated to remaining single for at least a year, maybe three, maybe 50 (my goal is to live to 105).

Fuck it all. I'm gonna break this system.

xoxoxo

Tinder was so much more fun than Bumble. I could swipe to my heart's content, not having to consider if I was going to have to start the conversation. I sat back and let the men chat me up first. Since I had so many people to meet and because it made me feel like a bad bitch, I decided to have back-to-back dates on Friday.

First up to bat was The Artist, slotted for 4 p.m. I rode the streetcar down to the River Market and walked over to Brown & Loe. I'd chosen it for its proximity to date two and because they had my favorite Framboise Raspberry Lambic on tap. He'd messaged me that he was at the bar, but when I walked in I couldn't figure out which guy was him. Then I recognized his glasses. Either he had not updated his pictures over the 20-pound-weight-gain or perhaps he photo-shopped them. He was sitting on the same exact bar stool Tantric Man sat at the week before. He was a bit shy, which was surprising after the sexy conversations we'd shared on Tinder. Of course saying, "I wanna stick my tongue inside you," when you are eyeball to eyeball with someone on a sunny afternoon would be weird even though he'd messaged those exact kinds of things. We talked about escaping religion then shared some dating horror stories. We kissed goodbye in the middle of the sidewalk at 5:30 in the afternoon. I felt that delicious sexual tension between us, as in his place was a few blocks away and he was hoping I'd come there, but it was time for me to go on to other adventures, i.e. date two of the night, The Liberal Marine.

I walked the block and half to Harry's and got a table on the patio. Liberal Marine had texted he was running late so I called my mom. A few minutes into the call, I saw a man who I thought might be him being escorted to a table then a text popped up, *I feel like a tool if I just walked past you.*

I had channeled my inner slut with cute chunky heels, shorts, and a lingerie top. I was wearing the good Victoria Secret bra that lifted the girls up for some fresh air. They like to be out and about sometimes. His floppy plaid shirt, Sports Clips haircut, and serial killer glasses set me back for a moment but then I looked past them and saw that The Liberal Marine was very cute. Sparkling blue eyes, close cut blond hair, a dimple in his chin, and a kind smile.

While it was a balmy evening for October, I've never seen that much sweat on someone's face who wasn't mowing the lawn or something. It dripped down his forehead throughout our drinks and apps. He kept swiping at it with a napkin. He bought me a tequila shot as promised. We talked about history as he was fascinated by it while I was fascinated to meet someone from the Ozarks who was so liberal. He didn't ask a lot of questions about me but I let it slide as I wasn't looking for a partner, just a fuckboy. I told him I was not going to be exclusive with anyone for at least a year. He found the honesty "hot" and said he was not a jealous person.

We were a little tipsy when we left the restaurant. Mere hours before I'd made out with The Artist a few blocks away and now Liberal Marine leaned in and kissed me. He said I had soft lips. More kissing ensued, just a few feet from the restaurant door. Again he exclaimed how soft my lips were. It was to become the running joke of the night. I decided to invite him over as those kisses were really nice, good lip pressure, just the right amount of tongue. Floppy plaid shirt be damned, this guy was hot.

As we walked to his truck, he complimented me on my ass. I had thought it was too big from my time with Hoppy who hadn't expressed appreciation for said ass in years, if ever, but this wasn't the first time a date had mentioned liking it in the last few months. At that moment, I cast off my old opinion and accepted that it was a good ass to have. He mentioned his truck had been having trouble starting. Surprise surprise, it didn't start now so we left it to take the streetcar. While we waited we kissed more, holding back in hopes of not permanently scarring the family standing a few feet away. A gentle rain started falling. By the time the streetcar arrived ten minutes later, he'd said my lips were soft close to a dozen times, once after each kiss.

Back at my loft we moved straight to the bedroom, lips connected as much as possible throughout the process of removing our clothes, falling on the bed where he moved from my lips to nibble my neck, then nip at my breasts, biting and licking them to little points then exclaiming at their beauty.

He took his time as he ran his tongue down my belly taking the curves slowly and carefully making his way to the folds, now throbbing from his ministrations, so ready for him to pay heed. Pay heed he did before he slid into me. We bucked together, bodies in heated rhythm reaching the pinnacle together quickly. We fell apart, breathing hard.

As we lay there recovering, the gentle rain turned into a full storm, thunder and lightning raged as we turned to each other and began kissing, starting up round two. It was past midnight when round two ended. The agreement had been that he'd go home to sleep. He begged not to be sent out into the raging storm since his truck battery was dead. I acquiesced, which meant I didn't sleep much as I wasn't used to having someone in my bed but I did get morning sex that started my Saturday off right. After scrambled eggs at City Diner, one of those great places with black and white tiles and cracked barstools, we jumped his truck. This had been a good test of having men stay over. I didn't like it. I wanted peaceful sleep, taking up the entire bed if I wished, and having my morning to myself. I recommitted to the ban I'd set for no sleepovers.

xoxoxo

I matched with a guy who said he had a Prince Albert piercing. I googled it, then ogled the results, agog when he sent a photo. The piercing goes through the hole in the tip of the penis. My god. For a moment I wondered what it would feel like to be pierced there, ouch, but the thought that sent that one scattering was what it would be like to ride it? I was getting a cold so we sexted. I told him all my rules: No married dudes. No Trumpers. No exclusivity. My cold hung on for several days putting a kibosh on meeting in person. He was my main virtual man. I found myself smiling at my phone in the way you do. I'm a sucker for guys who have a way with a phrase.

We were supposed to go out on Thursday but he texted he had a migraine. It was an entire week later before we could mesh schedules for a Wednesday evening since he had his teenagers over the weekend. I came home from teaching, so tired that I stripped and climbed into bed for a nap. While I wound down, I began reading all our messages on the app and then our texts. It took me over a half hour. I was ready for a catnap, then a shower, when I got a text from him that he could come over earlier.

I'm naked in bed reading all of our texts, I replied.

Stay right there.

I explained that no I wasn't going to stay right there, that I was going to take a shower and I had to let him in anyway as the building doesn't have the cool "buzz guests in" contraption.

I'm on my way.

I showered and then decided to be a bit naughty so I donned the thigh high boots I'd bought at the Goodwill for an upcoming Rocky Horror Picture Show event, a teeny black dress, and taking a page from Bumble Biker, traipsed down to meet him with no undies on.

He said he liked the boots.

He was cuter in real life and had some nice muscles.

And he smelled great.

We kissed in the elevator. Good kisser. Nice beard.

In my place we got to it. He stripped me except for my boots, gently pushed me down on the bed and went to town downtown. Holy mother.

I was then careful not to break a tooth on his piercing.

He brought out what I coined the Happy Meal prize kit. In a sammich bag he had condoms, lube, and a brand spanking new penis ring with a vibrator. I rolled the condom on, then the vibrating ring. While it was a novelty it didn't add that much to the experience, but it did add a little spark, literally. My thigh-high boots stayed on throughout, adding another level of interest to the whole thing.

Afterward we walked in the rain to The Peanut and talked for an hour and a half. I was telling him about Hoppy Sporty Sport and he listened. All the way through. And asked questions. He mentioned something about his family. When I asked about it he said, "Wait though, are you finished with your story?"

What guy does that?

I told him about my journey of sluttery. He high-fived me. We talked about some of his recent dates also. I know I will tire of this eventually, maybe, but right now I'm loving my life meeting all these new people.

xoxoxo

I did some math and realized that I had only been single for four months of my entire 54-year-old life. Unacceptable. I began brainstorming ways to remain single as I obviously had a commitment issue, as in too much of it. I'd been in only three relationships since I was 17 years old: thirty years with The Vexed Hillbilly, six years with Hoppy Sporty Sport, then three months with Cranky. At least I was on a downward trend. The next relationship should only last... about two weeks.

That means I should probably "break up" with The Liberal Marine as I'd only known him two weeks but we'd had two 15-hour dates, and a plethora, a veritable multiplicity of texts. He wanted too much. Although he said he was patient and not jealous, he wanted me to spend the night once a week. That was not going to happen. Goddamnit. I was trying to break the system. I wanted to flirt and be flirted with because it was fun and I'd never had that. The time was now. I wasn't getting any younger. I wanted to get it out of my system. I hoped, eventually, to have a relationship with someone who continued to flirt with me. I wanted to get to know lots of different types of men. I like men. Some are dildo heads but many are pretty interesting and I just think it's fun to meet them. I didn't have the energy for maintaining a relationship but why did I have to? I wanted to have lots of sex. I was enjoying sex. It was kinda like yoga I think. Or it had felt that way several times over the last few weeks.

I crafted some rules along with an update on my progress toward following them:

1. No staying the night.

This one was gonna be hard but it's important. Get some and then get out. Wake up in my own bed. Alone and do my thing. This staying the night leads to breakfast which leads to spending the day which leads to too much too soon.

Update: I am doing terribly with this. Liberal Marine stayed the night here and then I stayed the night at his place the next weekend. I have to get this UNDER CONTROL

2. **Wait one year to start anything remotely relationshippy. Maybe more.**

Still completely on board with this one.

3. **To keep things from becoming relationshippy only do hook-ups or established FWBs. No real dating.**

What is a date? What is an FWB? It says "friend." Are you a friend if you just have sex? But if you start doing friend stuff then you are dating aren't you? Helppppp.

4. **No dating apps.**

Ha! I think I downloaded Bumble that night. Then Boo made a Tinder for me. FAIL. But I'm not sure how I was gonna get FWBs or hook-ups without a dating app?

5. **Cool guys are in the friend zone. For at least a year. Only date people I don't like so I don't fall in love.**

Wait. I don't want to be with uncool guys so this one won't work. I either have to not date at all or I have to figure out a way to keep my distance.

6. **Start doing the things I actually want to do with my life instead of worrying about a damn man.**

I'm not doing well with this either honestly. I find myself waiting for texts to feel validated, which makes me think I may have to drop all of this shit and just be a person sans any men for a while. But can I do that? I have so much fun with it. If I can only keep it in perspective. Why can't I?

Let's be honest. It sounds like I need to not "date" anyone. Just do the deed and get out. This Liberal Marine is messing up my mojo and I don't want to hurt him. Damn it to hell. I want to be a slut for a year. I don't mean that in a pejorative way whatsoever. I think it's a fine choice. So how do I remain a slut and not fall in love?

xoxoxo

It wasn't the wisest decision. I'd been at my parents' house in the Ozarks all weekend and was driving back to Kansas City on Sunday afternoon. I realized it was early enough that I could fit in a date.

As I sped by the green pastures dotted with cattle, I began to think through my options. Prince A had his kids until eight so he was out. I'd had a couple of dates with The Banker, a first meet at SoT,[34] a favorite swanky whiskey bar where we'd made out on the patio and then football-game watching at a sports bar but I didn't feel comfortable reaching out for a booty call. (Although I had drunkenly done so the night I met him and he'd said he loved it even though he'd been asleep and missed it and he hadn't made sure my booty was called in the ensuing days.) Liberal Marine it was. I knew he'd been at a family Chiefs party all day and wondered about the state of his sobriety, which would affect his love-making abilities. Men mixed with copious amounts of beer don't make a great time.

I checked out the situation by texting, *How are you feeling?*

---

34 SoT was where Hoppy and I had planned to have our wedding reception. Yes he had planned it with me knowing it was never going to happen I guess. And yes, we had planned it without him actually asking me to marry him.

He had a whole text conversation with me and even said it was okay we lost the game because he was "a fan of adversity." I assumed a person who could text that would be sober enough for some shenanigans. I asked his thoughts on a booty call with arrival in about 45 minutes. He texted, *Come over. Please.* I set my maps to his place, told him I'd like to take a quick shower at his place, and headed that way.

He was high and drunk. He said he'd smoked twice and had nine beers. I'd just gotten in the shower when he climbed in with his clothes on. I didn't even have time to wash the parts I wanted to wash.

It was good skin-on-skin time. Great kissing. But the beers had affected him to where none of that good penetration was gonna happen. He didn't want me to go. He wasn't mean or forceful, just wanted me to stay saying, "All you have to say is get off me; I have to go." I finally did, after 2 $1/2$ hours. As I reflected the next few days, I was kind of angry. A little at him. But more at myself.

I have to change the pattern where I put dudes before myself. I've trained myself to live on what is available, not asking for what I need. The Judeo-Christian philosophy of being last is best is soaked into me. With the men in my life I automatically do that because that's what I do, everywhere. Work, family, friends, if something comes up I will think, "Do I have to have this?" and it's usually no. I'm beginning to see, at age 54, that this does not make a good basis for a relationship. Also the world is not going to fucking fall apart if I use my voice to ask for what I need, and just what I want.

xoxoxo

The Liberal Marine texted Monday to apologize, saying he was mad at himself. I told him I was upset he hadn't been forthright with how messed up he actually was, which shows my naivete because what drunk or high person knows how drunk or high they are and conversely will turn down great pussy being dashed to their door. I told him, again, that I didn't want to disappoint him about how much time I could spend with him as I wasn't going to be exclusive with anyone for quite awhile. He backed off and hasn't been blowing up my phone (which I missed a little bit).

I had planned to hang out with him the next Sunday but canceled after I woke up with a rager of a hangover from Saturday night shenanigans with Boo induced by not enough food and water and too much Fireball and dancing.

As the day wore on my hangover waned while my sex drive waxed, so even though I was still a bit nauseous and dizzy, I decided to rally. By the time I texted Liberal Marine to tell him I was alive again, he had already made plans, which is probably for the best. I also texted Prince A who couldn't believe I had "turned down dick" for a hangover and said he had one available, a dick that is. But when I asked him to drive it over to my place he said he had "wet sheets in the laundry." He's a wet sheet.

Prince A is playing me I believe. I told him when I was available through the next week and he said nothing. I asked Boo about it and he said if Prince A wanted to hang out with me he would. I deleted all his messages and felt better immediately. Deleting the messages was something like, "Hey I'm walking away from you by deleting all of this. You didn't reject me; I reject you first." It didn't make any sense to me either, but if a little thing like that helped me regain my balance then it was worth it.

The Liberal Marine must have been thinking of what he'd turned down the day before because his texts on Monday night were sweltering. From *I want you to kiss me like it's my very breath that's keeping you alive,* to *I want to feel you grind your hips into me while you pant for more,* finishing off with, *I'm torn between wanting to kiss your lips and catch your eyes looking into mine, or tossing you across my bed ripping off your panties putting a pillow under you and smacking your ass while I fuck you silly. I think I've decided I'll take both.*

The loins were on fire, both his and mine, so I texted the horny Liberal Marine at 4 p.m. on Tuesday asking him to come see me. He was on it. I had thought we could have sex, go eat, and then have more sex, but had not shared this plan. He texted he was starving, so I blew out all the candles in the bedroom and went out to help him find parking, which is a total bitch in downtown KC. He was wearing his hideous glasses but his hair was looking better than our first date because it grew out some. He had on a Delta Faucet hoodie so I was glad I wore a hoodie. We walked down to Milwaukee Deli and he made me laugh over beer and pizza. I told him my botched plan of sex-food-sex and he felt it to his core. He said to tell him the plan next time as he shook his head at me. Of course we did do ⅔ of the plan, food-sex. He's a goddamn good kisser, and sex is really good with some little bites and light scratches and just-right spanking involved.

xoxoxo

I deleted Tinder and closed my account in a fit of annoyance. I think turning 55 has aged me out of some people's searches. I don't look 55 and for sure don't act it. I could lie about my age like 85% of the men do. (I'm peering at the wrinkles on their face and it blatantly says 42.) I deleted Tinder but I added the Hinge app.

I started talking to Mike from Waldo and he seemed okay. Then one thing led to another and I'm putting on cute red panties to send him a pic, then my boobs, then my cute ass. (I didn't know it was cute. It better be as I almost tweaked my back holding the phone in the air behind me taking 25 shots before I liked one.) We set a date. The plan was to meet for drinks after his cable guy left at 6-ish.

I texted him at 3 p.m., *Hey I'm trying to decide between jeans and a dress.*

At 4:15 I queried if the date was still on as it had sounded like 6:30 was the probable time.

Sorry! I will be working until after 5:30!

Working? I thought he was waiting for the cable guy? I smelled a fish but kept getting ready. I shaved my legs and put on the good moisturizer.

At 6:30 I said Dude are we on or not? I'm going to go to a concert if not.

At 6:45 he texted, Just getting home. Have fun!

What the literal fuck? He wasn't a surgeon. I know surgeons can't text at work. But pretty much the rest of us can shoot off a quick 10-second text. Of course we can. So he just didn't. And then that whole cable guy thing. I told him he was rude and what the hell and please delete my pix. Then I asked if he'd planned on coming at all.

He said, *I thought you were going to a concert.*

Nooooo I was going out with you. I appreciate honesty even if you were on another date or happy hour or whatever. I don't care as long as I know what's up.

Nothing. And now he had pix of my face and boobs and ass, not all in the same picture. I'm not that dumb. But still. I was looking forward to talking with him and maybe having sex. I can't believe he didn't follow through just for the sex?

The Hinge app gave me a whole batch of men I had not seen, different from Bumble and Tinder which have the same exact dudes on them. A young man of 31 was messaging me before I had my filters set. He had a great bod and said I was on his bucket list. I liked that. I didn't like it a few minutes later when he asked me if "my pussy was tight." Excuse me? I didn't ask him if he had a small dick or if he lost erections. I said I'd had no complaints.

Then he said, *Well if it isn't tight I will use your asshole and cum in it.* I unmatched and blocked him and set my filter to age 40 and up. Fucking millennials.

The other rejection I'm experiencing is Prince A. He supposedly had to help his brother with a busted pipe last Friday and canceled our date. In a drunken weak moment on Saturday night (I'm going to have to delete numbers from now on), I sent Prince A a picture of my legs in fishnets when I was out and about. He immediately texted back asking how I was. I responded that I was out having a grand time with friends then I stripped his skin off for not texting this week. He said that douchebaggery was afoot. I said he'd need to make it up to me. He said he would. We shall see. If there's more douchebaggery, he's gone. He said he hoped we'd hang out soon. I sent him my open dates for this week. Of course he has not texted. What the hell with these guys? Don't leave me hanging. I decided I would text him and ask if he was ghosting me. Probably the exact wrong thing to do but I don't care. He's said nothing so far. So…

Fail.

On that note, men can suck a big one on this day. A rough week all around. A fuckboy, a no-show, and a ghoster. Triple assholes. A bit much.

Also it's been bothering me that I wanted to hang out with The Liberal Marine again and I can't. I'm not going to see anyone more than once a week. This will help keep me relationship-free. When he came in for the Tuesday night booty call there was a moment where our eyes met over dinner and it was too close for comfort.

I'm not going to pine after anyone.

xoxoxo

I handed my phone number to three men in the last 24 hours. Separately, bitches. That would be weird to a group.

Man #1

God he was so cute, curly brown hair and a great smile. Had shorts on so I could see his great legs. And he had a dimple. How do I know this? I sat next to him during breakfast yesterday at Happy Gillis. I heard him tell his friends he was 41 and that's when I perked up and really paid attention. I thought he was younger but 41... doable.

He was eating his overnight oats like.. well like I'd like him to eat me. Whewwww damn. I listened to everything he and his friends were saying, which was very easy because this was a teensy breakfast place and I was three inches away from him. I was reading my textbook waiting for my friend and placing my left hand just so. You know ,so he could see I was not married.

He didn't look.

I was waiting for my friend for our breakfast date which she didn't eat because she's starting that thing where you only eat in certain hours. Whatever. I enjoyed my humongous egg and bacon sammich. I don't care anymore if people want to eat or drink the same thing. I do what I want. Yes, I used to care and match people. I know. I'm a fucking weirdo.

I was coming off my rejection from being stood up Friday and night. Needed to jumpstart myself.

So I did.

I got my business card out of my backpack and slipped it under my napkin. I thought about giving it to his friends while he was gone to the restroom then decided that would be weird.

They all walked outside and were talking on the sidewalk. I saw him telling a story and swinging his hips back and forth wildly and laughing so hard. My friend had gone to the restroom. I probably wouldn't have done it if she were there watching. But she wasn't. So I grabbed my card, stepped out of the shop and handed it to him. All three of them said thank you. I think they thought someone left something. Nope, just me.

He hasn't texted. It's been 24 hours.

Oh well. I did it. Challenge accepted. Fuck rejection. I don't care. Gotta put yourself out there.

Man #2

My friend Eva and I went to Rocky Horror Live. I was wearing thigh boots and fishnets. I felt amazing even though she also had thigh boots and could be my daughter because she's 24 and she looks like Eva Mendes. I still felt cute even though her beauty is incredible and she's young and glowy.

We were at this dive bar before the show and I was watching this guy playing pool. He was kinda cute. Seemed like he was a little sad. I caught his eye a couple of times. His friend was boldly watching Eva, her cute cousin and me. But this guy was that broody sexy.[35] I got a pen from the bar. Eva's cousin Sassy had some paper. I wrote my number down and then Sassy asked my plan. I said I'd hand it to him as we left. She said it would be much spicier to hand it to him and sit back down. It's easy to hand it and walk out.

Hmmm... challenge accepted. I went right up to him and handed to him and asked, "Are you single?"

He's staring at this piece of paper with my name and number on it, "No Scarlett, I'm not." He seemed kind of sorry he wasn't single. He was nice about it and handed it back to me.

I smiled and took it back and said, "Oh well then," and went to the bar to get a shot.

Man #3

At the bar, I stood near a guy wearing a white Adidas jacket who'd acquired the bartender's attention earlier in the evening for us. We were at Zoo Bar, a dive that only cares about its regulars, an auspicious group of which he was a member and I was not. I asked him if I could get a shot for $6 as it was all I had (Luckily Sassy had given me a dollar.) It was a cash only bar. He thought I could, and if not he'd pitch in. Six bucks covered it and a tip. We were talking about age and he said it was rude to talk about. I disagreed and asked him how old he was. He said 36. I handed him my number I still had in my hot little hand and walked to my table in the other room.

He texted in the time it took me to walk there, about 30 seconds. He offered to buy me a drink but I was already toasty enough and we were headed out. Haven't heard from him this morning.

---

35 I know now that probably means he is a dick.

It was fun handing my number to three guys. I shall continue.

xoxoxo

I've commenced the year of sluttery. AT LEAST a year. I'm making it a year because I have a tendency to look at the glass as half full with men and then stay and stay and stay. Therefore I'm making myself date lots of people for a year. Giving myself a year feels doable. I need to see who the hell I am and what the hell I want. One month into it, I'm dating so much. Perhaps too much. But I want to, so I am. I can see a point where I might not, but maybe not. I'm dedicated to doing what I want.

However I do not want to hurt anyone. And there's the rub. When do I tell guys that I'm not going to be exclusive? If they ask, of course I tell them right off. The first month I told them in our first messages before we even met. Here's what I'm thinking though, a reason I shouldn't spill the beans quite so early, they all have different ideas of what an FWB is. If I say all this before they meet me then that could be killing some really great possibilities. At first I was thinking I would just run through a bunch of men and not see people more than once. But I'm realizing that it might be cool to really build the friendship part, to see how life is going and check in and send sexy texts and how ya doing and hang in there. Also I've been thinking that someone could make it through the fire of this year, maybe, and be a lifelong partner. You never know. Therefore this last week I was more reticent about sharing my sluttery.

Here's what I'm thinking for the rules of this:

#1 I am 100% honest, always.

#2 This means if they ask at any time what my goals

104

are, I immediately tell them my thoughts.

#3 I will stay on top of my feelings and what is being communicated and how things feel.

Drama, Drama, Drama

November 2019

Hmmmm... what is the maximum number of dates I can have with different men in a week and still go to work and grad school and still meet the bottom level of Maslow's Hierarchy? Let's try six...

Wednesday night: Sunglasses. I don't know much about this guy. He says he's 52, but I think he's older. We struck up a conversation about traveling to Italy. I am meeting him tomorrow night for dinner.

Thursday night, Halloween: The Liberal Marine. Can't wait to see him again. He makes me laugh. We are getting to know one another as we've hung out once a week for over a month now.

Saturday night, Prince A.: I texted him. My friends are disappointed in me. But I just wasn't done with Prince A. Really looking forward to seeing him again as the one date we had was too good. He's been sketchy on texting me and canceled our date a few weeks ago.

Sunday afternoon, Tantric Man or The DJ: Tantric man texted that he missed me and wanted to see me before our next scheduled rendezvous. He said maybe Sunday. The DJ, who I met at John's Big Deck for a first meetup drink last Sunday asked me out for the weekend. He actually asked, so he's first. Then if he falls through, Tantric is up to bat.

Next Wednesday, Happy Hour: The Poet: We have a first meet happy hour scheduled for next Wednesday. I was attracted to him because he was holding a notebook at an open mic in his Bumble photo.

Next Wednesday, Dinner: The Engineer: He's 35 and a cutie.

Well that's the round-up.

xoxoxo

I just texted Prince A asking why I should not tell him to fuck off. What's up with this mofo? And why am I still interested?

It's not because he's playing hard to get. It's because he's fucking hot...because the sex was great...because we went to dinner he really and truly listened and paid attention. He's funny and well-read. He is the only date to walk me to my door and escort me inside the locked part before leaving. When I told him I was enjoying listening to *Ready Player One* on audiobook on the road trip to see my parents he said it made him want me more... then he said not to share that with my family. Why would he care if he's never gonna meet them?

In a month though I've only had one date with him.
- He broke date one: migraine.
- We had a date nine days later.

• He texted less the next few days and when I asked why, he said he was mulling the FWB thing.

• He canceled the second date: brother's pipes had burst.

• He sent me a pic the next night while I was out with friends. The next day I invited him for a booty call but he had "wet sheets." I told him my avail dates. He ghosted for a week.

• He invited me to come over on a Tuesday. I had class.

• Wednesday when I texted that a date was canceled and I was so glad. Later he said I could have napped with him and I told him he had not invited me.

We set this date. He's been in constant contact all week. At 1 p.m. he texted: *Hey sugar, My Aunt from Colorado is in town on her way to Ohio. Can we please do each other tomorrow? I had no clue she was coming and have been threatened by my folks to not miss her. I'm super sorry. Please!!!???!!*[36]

I texted back, *I would, but I have plans tomorrow from 11 until 9 o'clock.*

Fuck ME!!!!!!!! That sucks!!

I said nothing for four hours. Then I sent, *Hey mofo, What's your Monday night look like*

No plans

Hmmmm... My class is canceled

Sweet

Angry at his "sweet" and not "Oh wow that's great! Let's get together!" Then I sent, *Ok.*

Waited another 30 minutes and sent, *Why should I not tell you to fuck off?*

He read it at 7:03 p.m. It's 8:35.

Motherfucker.

---

36 Is it just me or does this sound like a teenager's text rather than a grown ass man? Gross.

xoxoxo

The DJ asked me to a local movie premiere where the director would be doing Q & A. He parked in my loft garage and we took an Uber to the theater. I assumed because he was going to drink and didn't want to drive.

The DJ was around my height, like 5' 6", and solid. He had an interesting style with a cool black coat and very nice shoes. He needed to do some clipping on nose hairs. He isn't broke like I am, drives a nice car, and can pretty much do what he wants. He had a super sexy voice. He was smart and super interesting. I loved talking to him. This was the reason for the second date. The movie was cool. A friend of his met us there and was nice. The DJ made sure I was taken care of, opened doors and was very sweet. I'd worn my favorite new Lucky jeans and knew he was looking at my ass. I thought maybe he liked it. He told me later. He did.

We walked to Chicken & Pickle, a pickleball establishment, especially for street corn because he couldn't believe I hadn't tried it yet. He was right; it was tasty. It was so easy to talk to him that I revealed my year of sluttery. When I told him I was thinking of taking a class to learn a striptease chair dance, he almost lost it right there in the restaurant. We Ubered back to my place and started making out on the sidewalk. Someone walked by and told us to get a room. I decided he should just come up. The only reason I was iffy on it was that it was Sunday night and I had to get up so early. We got up to my place and he looked at my camera collection for a few minutes and said it was cool. We didn't spend much waxing lyrical about photographic equipment since we were already heated up from the sidewalk kissing. He was great with his fingers and his mouth so I was warmed up. Because he was so verbal, I got to hear this running commentary about how I tasted and felt. It's something that perhaps lots of women worry about. We had sex for a straight hour. I tell you these guys are long-lasting.[37] It's so crazy. He asked if I was a light sleeper. I said yes and asked why. He said he snored. I don't like people to spend the night anyway because I can't rest. He kissed me and left. I texted him and thanked him for the date. He said it was amazing and so was I. We made plans to have sex on his balcony.

xoxoxo

Prince A said he didn't mean to make me mad. I asked if he'd like to drive his horny ass down to see me on Monday. He didn't text back all Sunday although he'd read it at 8 a.m.

He texted Monday morning he would LOVE to come down. I said come on down. At 4:30, I asked if he was still coming and what time? I sent him a pic of my legs in the bathtub, then my see-through panties, then my cute bra as I was getting ready. He looked at the pix and text at 5:13 p.m.

And said nothing.

I called at 5:33. It went straight to voicemail. I called again at 5:43 and left a message asking if he was messing with me or if he was okay.

I believe I am blocked. The last text I sent has no Delivered line. Damn. I don't even get it. How did I read him so wrong? Here I sit in my cute jeans and my

---

37 Figured out later that many of my dates had a little help in this department from a pill, which is fine, I just didn't know that and they didn't reveal it at the time. I have no idea if The DJ did this or not, just speaking in general.

snakeskin boots and my see-through panties and I'm hungry. I guess there are just fuckers out there who'd rather fuck with you than fuck you? That makes no sense at all to me. I've felt shitty from our interactions so many times. And if he called and said his phone had died and he was sorry, damn it I'd believe him. He's not going to. I know his Facebook, but I'm not going there. I'm just so curious on the why of it. That is what is driving me crazy. Why? Did he think I was weird or didn't have good sex or didn't like the year of sluttery. He did though. He liked me and he liked the sex and he was cool. I can't make it work in my brain.

So… fuck Prince A.

I hope his pierced dick gets black and falls off.

xoxoxo

The Liberal Marine invited me to go to V's, a local Italian place in Independence. I drove to his place after work since the restaurant was near where he lived.

We knew if any clothing was removed we wouldn't make it out of the house so we kissed by the door then, breathing heavily, headed out. V's is a family place that was built in the 70s and they didn't change the decor. My favorite kind of place. He had an Italian beer while I got my favorite old-fashioned. He ordered bruschetta for us. We told the server we just wanted to enjoy our drinks. She went away and left us. We drank and talked and ate this wonderful bruschetta and then we started touching hands.

After fifteen minutes of this touching, looking into each other's eyes and trying to talk, I said perhaps we should just get our food to go. He whole-heartedly agreed. I told the server we'd decided to get out of there which probably didn't surprise her. She got that food out fast.

We drove to his place and I took a quick shower, put on my fishnets, black lace nightie, and some blue snakeskin heels. I gave him a BJ in this so he could get an eyeful. After we were satiated in the bedroom, he warmed up the fettuccine for me, then sat on the counter and watched me eat. He wanted to eat later. We kissed and started it all up again and I stayed an hour longer than I meant to, but it was fun. My legs were sore the next day like I'd run two miles.

xoxoxo

I had left-swiped the Brit when he popped up on Hinge a few weeks before, but then Hinge said we were compatible so I swiped right then made a joke about it. He asked me out for the weekend but I had plans so we had set a date for next Sunday, eons away.

We were messaging and he asked if I could squeeze in a happy hour as he was leaving for a business trip the next day. I thought this was a great idea. I love surprise Monday night dates. I picked Parlor, where I'd met Tantric a few times. As I walked up, I saw him peering out of the second story window looking for me. He was cuter than his photos.

We laughed and held hands and kissed. I felt comfortable with him in the first hour. I snuggled under his arm on the couch and laid my head on him while we talked. We were there for two hours but it felt like ten minutes. We plan to hang out again on Sunday when he gets back.

I've decided it's okay to like people rather than just hangout with people I don't like so I don't get attached. I just don't want to date only one person and I don't want to live with anyone. I told my counselor that I don't want anyone to get hurt. She said that's not really my place as I can't control who gets hurt. However I don't want to lead anyone on. So far it's been fine.

xoxoxo

I matched with Baby Ginger and quickly realized he thought he was a hot ticket simply because he's 20 years younger than me.

He messaged on my Tinder photo, *No fucking way you're 51. 37, tops.*

I told him I was in fact 55. He said, Y*ou're a certified fucking smokeshow.*

He asked if I was into younger guys and said he had a funny feeling he could *end up being into this*. I said I could be into younger guys and that, *Younger guys have been in-to me.*

Good. I think I can count myself amongst them. Let's see if you can keep up. Are you looking for something serious? he asked, missing my joke. (you know.. about younger guys being "in" me…)

Oh, I'll keep up, I assured him. *And no, just looking for fun.*

He said we could have some fun and once again he had a funny feeling we could get into some mischief.

I asked to schedule a drink. This gets a meetup and clears out guys who just want to message. Our schedules were both crazy this week so we are looking at next Tuesday. He compared me to Mrs. Robinson. And once again felt funny, *I have a funny feeling we may end up seeing a lot of each other soon.*

We took things to text and did a bit of sexting at bedtime, a few pix were exchanged. A challenge was offered up of who can best the other one in sex.

He's not that fun on text. We will see where it goes. I'm not holding my breath.

xoxoxo

I matched with The Poet on Bumble. He's messaged the fewest number of words I've ever seen so I couldn't get a great sense of who he was but I gave him a chance because he writes, which is ironic I suppose.

We met up on Wednesday afternoon in Westport at my favorite whiskey bar, Julep. We talked about writing. He was not flirty at all. I kept the convo going mostly but he did ask some things and it was a pretty great conversation in the end. I liked that he asked our server's name and used it. I had paid for my drink and appetizer before he got there somehow knowing he wasn't gonna want to pick up the check as he's younger, 37. I was right. When the check came it was only his, but he didn't know that because he didn't pick it up. I finally told him I had paid for mine already. He didn't protest.

I had a date with The Liberal Marine at 6 so I put my coat on at 5:30. He walked me to my car. We passed the restaurant where Coffee Meets Bagel Married Guy and I had dinner back in May so I told The Poet about it and how he had said the L-word after our first date. He asked if I had superpowers. I said I had let all my feminine powers out on the date. I demonstrated how it went down. I grabbed The Poet's tie and pulled him close and kissed him. It was a good kiss. He was into it. He asked me if that had really happened or had I just wanted to kiss him. I said it really happened. We kissed more by my car and it was very nice. He mumbled something. I realized he'd said he wanted more. I stepped back a bit, raised my eyebrows and assessed him. He wanted it right then. So there was some fire in the ice cool Poet after all. But I had a date with Liberal

Marine in 20 minutes. Got. To. Go. I said we'd pick this up on date two.

He strolled away and adjusted his pants. Within five minutes a text popped in, *Nice* and a winky emoticon. I sent back a smooch and he said, *Don't go falling in love.*

I said, *Me? Or was that for you?*

For you.

Ah.

Mmmmmhmmmm

I'm protecting my heart. No worries.

Good deal.

If anything I figured he would fall for me. I laughed aloud in the car as I headed to the date with Liberal Marine.

The Liberal Marine messaged, *Fuck sticks I really need a handful of hair,* so we set up this date. I met him on the sidewalk, a bit late from the date with The Poet. We went up to the loft and kissed. I noticed he wasn't his normal self. He began feeling worse so we cuddled for two hours. He finally left, so disappointed about the night.

After he left, I saw that Baby Ginger had texted asking if I was having a good time on my back to back dates. I texted him back the next morning and said they were good. He said maybe I didn't need him then. Well I don't need him. I don't "need" any of these people. I need my family and friends. But not Baby Ginger for damn sure.

I was nice. I said, *Need or Want,* or something like that.

I then sent him a selfie to which he replied he'd like to choke my pretty mouth with his dick. I said that didn't sound fun to me, but that I was horny because one date got sick last night. He asked what happened and if he was "70" and why couldn't he get hard?

Stupid child man. I said things happen and we had naked cuddle time, which he mocked. I said I'd rather have a nice naked cuddle than be choked. He said I was too vanilla for him. That's fine if we don't match up in the BDSM department, but don't be a dick about it.

Then I thought... Wait, am I vanilla? I don't feel vanilla.

I've enjoyed anal a couple of times when people warmed things up and knew what they're doing. I enjoyed being spanked while being taken from behind. It is fun when a man got heated pushing me against the wall or held my hands. I adore feeling the graze of some teeth. I've taken some chances in public, had sex on a couple of balconies in Mexico, and bared my breasts on the beach. I even enjoyed when Tantric Man, whom I trust, placed his hand on my neck and squeezed lightly which I did not know I would like. But I'm not into actual pain or total domination. I'm not sure that makes me vanilla though.

I did some research and vanilla means different things to different people. I guess I am vanilla to Baby Ginger. I'm okay with that. We are just not on the same page. I'm thinking about another guy I matched with on Tinder a few months ago and never met because something about him scared me when he called me "Honey."[38] Maybe because he didn't even know me? I'm not into being scared. I'm into connection and fun so yeah I guess I'm kind of vanilla at this point. Whatever it means, Baby Ginger ain't gonna be tasting any of this creamy goodness.

xoxoxo

---

38 This is The Neighbor in book two: *The Year of Discovery.*

I'm not a loser if I'm home on a Friday night. I'm not. Really. Right? I had a wonderful happy hour with a girlfriend whom I haven't gotten to hang out with for months. She is one week single so we talked about dating apps for a moment. She's 24 and one of her bangers is 44, whilst I am 54 texting a 34-year-old.

It seems the early 30's and the 50's want me, while everyone wants her. And no wonder. A platonic male friend of mine is late 40's and he wants all the twenty-somethings until they won't look at him. He says he's trying to get it all in now. I understand that twenty-something flesh is much firmer. But I'm also wondering other than firmer flesh what they would have over my 55-year-old ass? I love hanging out with Gen Z's and millennials. They are my friends but I think my friend is kinda missing the boat and something's twisted up. Yes I want to bang a few 34-year-olds, just for funsies but that's it. There seems such a gap to bridge for true connection.

I got home from happy hour and mulled whether to work out or take a nap. The nap won. I first downloaded Hook-Up Dating and put up a profile thinking I might want a quickie later. But I didn't talk to anyone. I woke up hungry and kind of cranky. I knew there wasn't much in the kitchen. There were bars with food merely a block away but I had no pants on and it did not sound good to put them on AND WALK OUTSIDE in the coldish air. I considered it. Also considered just starving and staying in bed another twelve hours. I texted The Fireman the details of my situation. He said he was in the same boat, had just consumed 10 tacos and was miserable and sleepy on a Friday night. Well then. What I wanted was a man to bring me his penis and some food. This should be a thing. Perhaps I should start that company..

Booties for Foodies. (Big juicy booties with gourmet foods)

Or *Sexy Pecs 'N Mex* (yeah baby, you got it)

Dicks 'n Delivery (all the food choices, like a sexy Postmates)

I feel very mature as I am eating tuna and crackers and I have pants on now.

Man Update

- Tantric Man is on the schedule for next Thursday. He's looking forward to it as am I.
- The Poet is doing one-word texts and will not be receiving a come-and-get-it from me. He will have to move his millennial ass.
- I texted Hoppy and told him I worry about him sometimes. He said he's fine.
- A cutie close to my age matched with me on Hinge and was super sweet. He said I was his first match, he'd joined two hours before and he was so happy to talk with me. Warning bells. When I asked what he wanted from Hinge he said, "The one." Well fuck. I told him that I was not exclusive and he stopped talking to me.[39]
- A sexy guy from another city who works with concert stuff matched earlier today and wanted to hang out but I had work then and he has work now. He was up front and said he was just out for fun, and I said so am I. He said he'd please me and when I asked how, he claimed to be a good lover. No message since like 10 a.m.
- A cute tattooed 35-year-old man has been messaging but it's pretty slow.
- An artist who lives nearby got annoyed last weekend

---

39 This is the kind of behavior that could get me kicked off Hinge, the "relationship" app.

when I messaged, "No worries." He said everyone has worries. I explained it meant for him not to worry about whatever we were talking about. No message all week then today practically asked himself over to my hot tub. I thought what the hell and invited him. He said, "Oh girl, that's like a third or fourth date." Okay. Whatever.

- I'm seeing The DJ tomorrow.
- I'm hanging with The Brit on Sunday. He's been very attentive on text on his business trip. I considered flying out to Arizona to hang with him at the pool. If he'd bought me a ticket, I'd have a sunburn right now. But that's crazy. So I'm here with my tuna and crackers and cracking the books.

xoxoxo

I've not had a date like today ever in my whole life. I didn't have to plan anything. The DJ asked me out, then surprised me with where we were going for lunch. When I asked what to wear he said Scarlett-style, meaning what I felt like (I changed three times.) He opened the car door for me, the whole date. He complimented me on my outfit and at one point even my cheekbones, which no one has ever done. He put my arm in his to walk with me down the street.

The place was so perfect, a crepes place called Chezelle Creperie in the Westside neighborhood. It was fun ordering because we looked at the menu together and discussed all the choices. I wanted to be outside. He moved tables and made it happen. We kissed. We held hands. We looked into each other's eyes. He has these amazing green eyes. We talked and listened to each other. It was so satisfying eating that good food. We went into a little shop and then a pop-up shop outside and I bought the cutest vintage case I'm going to use for a jewelry box. I wanted him. But he had places to go and people to see. He leaves for a trip and won't be back for two weeks. He has a date tonight. I'm glad he could tell me.

Later I texted, *That was the best date from beginning to end. Thank you. I hope you have fun tonight and meet the love of your life*[40] *and we'll have a threesome some night when we are all drunk and be friends forever. Here is a photo to remember me on your trip.*

Then I sent the boobies. I have a vixenish look in my eyes and you can see my face wrinkles. Who fuckin' cares? I'm his home screen, for now.

xoxoxo

Challenges for this year[41]

1.Have video sex.

Met: May September, October, November… (Normal operations were interrupted for Cranky Pants.)

2. Send nudes.

Met in May, September, October, November...

3. Have sex with a guy off HUD, HookUp Dating.

Met September 2019 with Big Guy, the night before I officially broke up with Cranky.

4. Initiate the first kiss.

Met: May with Coffee Meets Bagel, November with The Poet. Maybe others, not sure.

5. Give a guy my number.

---

40 I believe he did meet the love of his life that night for which I've received no credit, thank you very much. And as for the threesome, eh, I don't think it's my jam.

41 Like a true listmaker I put some things I'd already done because I wanted credit.

Met in May with Trivia Man and three guys on October 26.

New challenge: Flirt with man and give him my number. Don't just awkwardly thrust it at him and run away.

6. Go on back-to-back dates.

Met: May, September, November.

7. Eat at a bar by myself.

Met September, October and November.

New challenge: Go to a bar with live music by myself.

8. Go to a concert by myself.

Met October.

New challenge: Go to a GOOD concert by myself.

9. Join a group that cycles or hikes.

10. Do an open mic at a comedy club.

xoxoxo

I was doing well. I am woman, hear me roar and all that. I walked jauntily to a local place and sat at the bar by myself and read a book and ate. I came home and no one was talking to me so I felt lonely.

The DJ is on a date. I'm not going to bother him. I texted The Liberal Marine to see if he's okay. No response. Even the guy on an oil rig ignored me. I was swiping on Hinge and Cranky Pants popped up because I said age was not a "Dealbreaker." (Also some goddamn 23-year-olds liked me, what the fuck. I'm not a circus act here. I put Dealbreaker back on.)

There he was. I figured it would happen. I wondered if he saw my profile. I wondered if he hated me. I looked at his happy face and felt sad. We had some really good moments, some laughter, I said I loved him. We smoked cigars and danced on his balcony. There was his smiling face. I hadn't felt sad about him until now. I knew the alone-at-home-on-a-Saturday-night was adding to it but also that it was okay to feel a little sad. It didn't mean I was supposed to be with him. I swiped left.

xoxoxo

The Brit asked me out for lunch when he got back from his business trip. He had flirty texted throughout the week so I was looking forward to our date. He mentioned a new record player so I had asked if we could listen to records. I did want to listen to records… while doing other things. Lunch lasted over two hours with so much talking, including a full explanation of the game of cricket.

After lunch, he drove us to his place five blocks away. I mocked him for driving that distance. I chose U2's *Joshua Tree* since it was a longer album to give a bit more time to get into things but he didn't need it. We started making out post-haste. He mentioned that his teenagers would be there later. I asked when. We had an hour and fifteen. Not much time. Best get to it. So we did.

His body was so different from anything I'd been with. He was solid, barrel-chested. His biceps were quite amazing. He was a wonderful kisser. He pleasured me with his mouth, then I reciprocated and he quite enjoyed it. I like it when men are vocal in their appreciation so I know they are enjoying what I'm doing. Sex was grand. We finished and were cuddling then things got started up again. That time we got to my current favorite position, from behind, and a bit of spanking.

I was putting my clothes on when he said, "I err umm think you may have the condom," whilst looking down at his naked penis. I laughed, went to the bathroom, did a quick swipe and found nothing. I got out of there as his kids were due soon. He had offered to drive me but it was a sunny day and I love walking. I may have passed Victoria's Secret and dropped $100 but they were having the 10 panties for $35 sale. This is why I don't go to the Plaza.

When I got home, I was talking to my newly single 24-year-old girlfriend and remembered the lost condom.

"Oh hey I think I have a condom inside me. Is that a big deal?" She lost it. She told me that first of all my life was insane and secondly that I needed to get that thing out of me post-haste. I began dedicated search number one which took about three minutes.

Nothing.

I searched for tips on the interwebs and learned I was supposed to bear down WHILE relaxing. What the literal fuck? That is impossible. Some man wrote that bullshit. I attempted it. I squatted like they said, balanced, and tried to relax while jabbing my fingers around inside me as far as possible.

Nothing.

More research. I took a bath and stabbed my fingers around while in the bath.

Nothing.

I began to research exactly how serious the problem was.

Would I die before morning? No. It said no. Okay, good.

Would I be poisoned from latex as my little girlfriend said? No. The Interwebs said no.

I saw a tip to lube up your finger and tried that. I did get farther up there but still…

Nothing.

A few weeks before at a regular checkup my gyno

had said my cervix was way the hell up there, so I guess there's a lot of depth? This is why I thought it could be still lurking in there. I texted The Brit and asked him to look again. He was with his teens. He texted back an hour later and said he would do a deep check. I said I'd been doing a deep check for two hours! In the meantime I emailed work that I wouldn't be coming in. Obviously I didn't tell them I had a condom inside me and must visit the gyno for removal of said condom.

The Brit came back on text. He'd found it. It was hanging off the bike pedal by his bed![42] How the hell? I do not know how the condom flew through the air to the bike pedal. I then had to email my co-workers that I could come in and that the "family emergency was averted."

xoxoxo

Tantric Man and I have our little routine down now. He picks me up in his sports car, almost always a half hour late. He lets me know but now I know it's his normal. We head to Brown & Loe, a local eatery that sources food from area farmers. I get the Framboise Lambic, he orders the Luponic IPA. We split the meatloaf, mashed potatoes, and green bean dinner.[43] It's the perfect amount to feel satiated but not too full for the yoga sex to come. This will be our third "sex" date. Last time he put his hand on my throat and went for the back door but he had warmed everything up so it felt surprisingly good.

---

42 Isn't this a funny image? Assuming when we switched positions it flew off. I guess? It seems to break the rules of physics.

43 It sounds like we are a hundred years old. You can laugh at the idea of meatloaf pre-sexy time.

After dinner we went back to my place and post-haste got to it. We know it's going to be hours; better get started already. The surprising thing is that there aren't many preliminaries but I'm excited to be with him so it doesn't matter. I'm ready. This time he said he was in charge but to let him know if I wanted something in particular. This sounded interesting so I nodded. I was having trouble fully relaxing. I think I was wondering when he'd go for the back door. I knew he would as he did last time and for some reason this is the end-all be-all for dudes. Why is that?

I'd done it maybe three times in my whole life before Tantric Man and then twice now with him. Last time was okay, a bit of discomfort the next day but the experience had been worth it. He went for the back door and I allowed it as it was fun last time. This time it was too long and too forceful but I didn't stop it. I didn't realize in the moment how it was going because I was trying to have fun. I realized when we stopped. But still didn't say anything. Then we had round two of normal stuff. I was just trying too hard.

We talked afterward. He said I was middle of the road on being open or something like that. I guess that depends on if you are talking averages of the women in the United States or the women he hangs with who are poly and perhaps kinkier or more experienced than me. My body is an instrument for the knowledgeable to play. If I'm not there, it ain't because I'm not open. It's because things weren't prepped properly.

I know this because of Cranky. We could have sex for an hour, take a short break and start up again. I would literally soak the bed. So I know what's possible. No one has gotten there with me before or since. Yes, that bothers me. Yes, I want that again. No, I don't want to be with Cranky because we didn't have enough outside of the bedroom.

Tantric Man is knowledgeable and I did have fun. It's not his fault I didn't speak up but today he texted to say how much fun last night was.

It was fun. However recovery was not fun in the anal region today, I texted.

In so many ways we are pushing your body beyond what it is used to. That is part of an adjustment process. With time, your body conditions at this level of intensity. Kind of like a runner who needs to build up endurance to run a marathon. Last night with me on top behind you, it was as if you were conditioned for one mile but ran five miles. Your body felt it afterwards.

I was feeling a bit of bullshit detection but perhaps my sore anus was making me feel bitchy. I knew that I never wished to feel this way again down there. I replied, *Hmmmm. Will think on that.*

Yeah, same as the hydration and muscle cramps. All part of the learning process. But you will get there quickly. Once you no longer worry about those things then you can relax into the experience even deeper. Like yoga (I had told him my yoga idea). *You can go deeper into the poses. The deeper you go, the more powerful the sensation.*

Then he sent Chicago's *You're the Inspiration* and said he remembered dancing to it in sixth grade and how he really liked the girl. Then, *Perhaps there is some symmetry two decades later for you. I can be your writing inspiration and you can dance with me as if you never want the song to be over.*

I have lots of writing inspiration. I've mentioned he's arrogant but confidence is sexy. Too much isn't, but there's a fine line there. I said, *I like that song. Still not happy with the sore butthole situation though lol.*

I get it. (I mean do you though?) *I find it quite funny! I hope you can laugh with me as this makes a good memory.*

This does not make a good memory. I was at work and it hurt all day. It was uncomfortable as all hell. I said, *I will purchase a strap-on so you may enjoy it also!*

Sounds like an adventure! What are the odds you can actually maneuver something that big?

I laughed.

He sent a funny meme.

A couple of hours later I said, *Still hurts. Worried about farting. What* might *come out.*[44]

He said, *I guess you can't fart. Which will make you feel bloated. I just farted. Did that help? Maybe what you need is round two.*

God no. Nothing is touching that area for awhile or everrrrr.

He, two hours later: *I guess this is what you get for being so cocky! Maybe what comes around goes around?*

Me:

He, one hour after that: *Want to talk on the phone?*

Nope.

He, two more hours later, *Are you mad at me?*

Yes but I'm writing right now.

He: *Ok, you write. And hopefully accept my apology for whatever I did. It wasn't intentional.*

I realized that I did not convey my actual pissed-offness at the situation and made it all funny and light, oh hahahaha I am so goddamn sore and isn't it funny? It isn't funny and I'm upset.

What he's talking about with the whole "cocky" part is that I told him he's the first man to "best" me. That I usually can outlast every man I've been with. I'm ready to go again and again. He did best me. He did love that to pieces. My legs were cramping and I just couldn't keep going. He won.

But not really.

---

44 Yes, I actually texted this which shows you how much I really didn't care what he thought of me. I waffled on whether to include it as it is fairly awful but in the end ;) I decided to leave it here for your groaning pleasure.

He left and I had a little meltdown and then I've been sore. I'd rather have less intense sex and feel good after. This was not worth it.

xoxoxo

Friday nights are when I feel I should celebrate the week and have a grand time. I don't care to be home all the other nights but Friday hits me hard. It happened again this week. I had asked a couple of girlfriends to go to a concert with me if I could get last minute cheap tickets and neither texted me back. I was proud of myself for telling them that this bothered me and they both apologized. I would normally just think I wasn't as interesting as what they chose to do or something like that.

I took a nap and decided I was too broke to be going to a concert. So broke. So very broke. I was kind of teary that I was alone and a sad sack of shit. And poor.

I did have enough moolah to take myself down to a local bar. I went in and the bar was full except one seat squished between two dudes. I hesitated and he asked what was up and pushed the seat out so I sat. He was drunk and saying that weirdos in New York always came at him, a naked one recently or something. I was uncomfortable but not showing it. Not about the story but just him in general. I ordered a cider and then realized my wallet was in the pocket of the jacket I had just changed out of, back in my loft. Great.

I said I'd go get my card, and explained to the bartender I'd changed jackets. I hadn't put my lips on the can but he'd opened it already. He nodded. I left.

And didn't come back. I didn't want to. It's okay. Someone got a free cider.

Instead I went to The Quaff after I got my card. I

sat at the bar, felt teary again so I texted my girlfriend, the 24-year-old recently single hottie. She said lean into it. It was okay to be sad sometimes. The same thing I'd told her the week before. The things we know but have to hear from each other. I then consumed a huge cheeseburger and felt better.

Back at the loft later, a Tinder message came in from The Mail Man. He had a funny line about putting it in your box on his profile and he looked interesting, as in hot. I liked that he messaged me more than two words and he asked me straightaway to get a coffee or drink. Shocking, as most men on Tinder message one or two words and then ghost.

I said I'd love to. Then he asked to meet that night. I thought what the hell, let's do it. It was 8 p.m. I was ensconced in a warm loft with pjs and no bra. I put on my cute jeans and push-up bra and left my place to DRIVE to a Chez Charlie, a dive bar I'd not been to. I beat him there and got a whiskey diet. It was only three fucking dollars. In addition to the dive bar prices, the decor was frozen in 1972, my favorite kind of bar. There was a birthday party with a bunch of middle-aged people; one dude was actually wearing an awkward dollar store hat. Dart boards everywhere, a vinyl bench running all the way around the side. This is his very favorite bar in all of Kansas City. We are simpatico on what a good bar consists of.

The Mail Man gets there and is... different. Just really different from the men around here. Reserved maybe? I kept trying to draw him out. It seemed he was nervous. We are both working on open mic stuff so we talked about that. He bought a place recently; so we talked about that and about why I love living downtown so much. We bonded over our hatred of the asshole white privileged people of this city. He was fresh off a ten-hour day and had to work the next morning but made time for this drink. I sensed a kindred soul. He was getting ready to tell me a story then said he didn't want it to be a red flag. It worried him I could tell, but he still told it. It involved brass knuckles and some drug dealers who'd been trouble on his street where he'd recently moved. Twas an awesome story.

I told him about Baby Ginger and he was actually shocked. Then he said I should've led him on a bit and told him to meet me in the most expensive hotel in the city and then not show. Funny. But I wouldn't do that as it is too scary to provoke people. It's scary enough being a woman.

A guy walked over and put his darts on the bar to return them. Mail Man got this twinkly look on his face and snagged one of them. He then got the attention of the guy at the end of the bar to lower his head a bit then threw the dart on the board when the players weren't looking. They didn't notice until they were taking the darts down and were just befuddled as to where it came from. The best part to me was the look on the Mail Man's face, this mischievousness, which I tried to tell him but he thought I was weird I think. That's okay. It's a writer thing I think. Or a woman thing maybe?

It was late so we headed out to the sidewalk. I gave him my number and we hugged goodbye. I texted and said how much fun I had and mocked his Tinder song, a weird country hiphop situation. He texted back that he had a fun/nice time (yes just like that fun/nice.) He said the song was not really his shtick (yes shtick) but thought it fitting for the area then that he should prolly change it as it was for the summer. (Yes prolly.) I ain't the grammar police.

Hoping he will text but I'm booked back to back to

back through the next eight days. However I'm going out with friends to a bar tomorrow night and would invite him if he asks to hang out.

xoxoxo

I told my inner circle that The DJ was a good friend because he treats me like he cares about me and my thoughts and thinks I'm cool as shit.

So I told The DJ about it, *I told them that I think you and I will be great friends until the day we die, that if my kids or sister were not available, I feel I could call you at 2:30 a.m. and you'd be there for me.*

He responded, *As long as we are still fucking each other my dear, count on it.*

That hit me like a punch in the face.

My first thought was I have this all wrong then. He wasn't what I thought. It was about the vagina after all. Not me. But wasn't right, I didn't think.

I said, *Ahhh but what if we were not. I'm probably jumping to conclusions as I do lol. We shall see. I do want to (fuck) but thought if you or I ended up in a relationship (with someone else) we might still be friends.*

I will always respect you and help you if I can, but I have friends already. I'm looking for something that's different... serendipitous.

He had friends. Didn't need my friendship. Huh.

I called Seester.

She said, "He's only in it for one thing, not the friendship."

Then we both said, "That's sad," at the same time.

She said, "We have to remember most people are assholes."

"I thought he wanted both friendship and romance. It hit me hard as I hold friendship as something that

131

transcends romance, at this point anyway," I said.

"That isn't right as he clearly said he has friends. He doesn't say what it is that is different that he's looking for. I assume the FWB thing and if the b stops then it's done."

I said, "Perhaps he doesn't want the friend zone?"

"He doesn't want you as a friend. He says that. Perhaps he only wants benefits."

"So if he's not fucking me he won't talk to me right? He said he empathized and admired my journey."

"And so it is. But he's not in it for the long haul friendship."

I texted him back that my sister and I are trying to figure out if he's an asshole. He says that will be a lifelong question, *But I will answer it for you.*

I said I was trying to understand and he said I was understanding. I said my vagina was more important than friendship but no he doesn't want a friend.

He: *Just as important.*

Me: *Which feels as if I'm not good enough to be your friend.*

He: *Hmmm why*

Me: *Without the sex you don't wish to be friends, which means you aren't interested in my friendship. But I think perhaps you are shooting for both. Maybe.*

He (of course): *I am shooting for both. With you.*

Me, an hour later: *So wait. You were going to tell me if you are an asshole I think.*

He: *I can be an asshole but I'm not an asshole.*

He doesn't want my friendship. He wants all of me. Yeah okay. I get that. Damn it. Is that admirable? To not be placed in the friend zone?

I don't like the way he said it at all, "As long as we are fucking." I do not like that. But in the long run I suppose that is what separates relationships.

There's just fucking.

The Year of Sluttery

There's just friends.

There's fucking and friends.

So... I carry on and whatever happens happens. I'm not giving anything up right now. He's not asking me to. Yet.

xoxoxo

The Poet arose from the ashes to text, H*ow's it going?* Epic. It had been two weeks since I last saw him. We texted back and forth about food then he said, *Home alone?*

Yes. I live alone.

Thinking smiley emoticon from him.

Ah. You are thinking about something. I wonder

Mmhmm.

Are you thinking you could come over?

If invited.

You are invited.

Oh, smile emoticon.

Parking is a literal bitch. But I have faith in you.

Gee thanks.

I sent my address and said I would have to come let him in.

I would hope.

I don't have a buzzer.

Ohk

20 minutes went by. In that 20 minutes I took a shower, put on cute undies and a sexy bra, cleaned up my place, and lit candles.

Is this like an open invite lol, he texted.

What does that mean lol, I respond.

lol like I just tell you I'm coming over and you're like okay?

I was a bit confused, *Ah. Hmmm. I'm a fairly open person but I do have plans often. And sometimes I am tired.*

He said, *Very good. I like scheduling.*

Is your ass headed over here lol, because I expected him at any moment.

Not tonight.

Wait. What? Why did he ask if I was home alone?

So did I misunderstand you? It seems you asked for an invite. And got one.

I thought you were giving me info for future use.

Wait. What?

I said, *I thought you were headed over. I took a shower and cleaned up my place a bit and lit some goddamn candles.*

Well damn.

Not sure how we got our wires crossed.

Shit.

I even put the new Victoria's Secret bra on lol. Lmao. I swear.

Stop it.

I did!

Fuck.

I sent a picture of the bedroom with the candles lit. *I'm not kidding. Crack me up.*

He: *Nice*

It is nice. I don't even know how a writer has such bad communication skills.

Me: *Go back and reread the texts. And show me where it isn't tonight,* rolling eyes emoticon.

He: *I'm sorry I'm sorry. I'll make it up to you.*

(Which reminds me The Brit promised some sort of make-up for my deep condom search.)

Me: Tapping fingers GIF

He: *Promise.*

xoxoxo

I'm not sure I could have created a more perfect Sunday morning. It began with relaxing yoga at Yoga

Patch, a place that didn't intimidate me. I am always the least bendy in a yoga room but I had found a place I felt comfortable, a place that truly welcomed all levels of fitness and all the kinds of people. I got so much out of it that I overcame my fears and didn't care that I was the "worst." I stopped to grab coffee and a breakfast sandwich at Crows Coffee Waldo, a favorite cafe, on the way to my storytelling group. The group included seven of us, four who flowed in and out and three of us who were there every time. Because of them, I had found the joy in writing again. Sunday mornings had been so many different things through my life but none feeding my body, mind, and soul the way this morning had.

As a child, the First Baptist Church bus had picked up my sisters and me for Sunday School. We mostly learned about brave holy men with a few sprinkles of women whose stories showed us what to be and not to be: Eve, whose rebellion lived on as a curse for all women; Ruth, who was a quiet hard worker; Mary, the virgin mother of Jesus; and Mary Magdalene, the impure woman who washed Jesus' feet with expensive oil and her tears. After Sunday School we'd skip the regular service, traipsing out to the street corner where Dad would pick us up. We'd grab the Sunday paper before heading home to help Mom get Sunday dinner on the table, fried chicken, mashed potatoes, green beans, fruit salad (canned fruit with whipped cream), white bread and butter all washed down with sweet iced tea.[45]

Sundays with The Vexed Hillbilly had begun with breakfast for the family, getting children ready, and three hours of church. Back home I made Sunday dinner (similar to my mom in that there was meat,

---

45 Told you I was from the Ozarks.

vegetable, potatoes, bread and Country Crock). Most Sundays I'd read the paper and take a nap before the scaries hit in the afternoon about work on Monday. Many of those years I bundled the kids into the car and took them to Sunday night church, then again Wednesday night, resulting in at least a half dozen hours of our free time spent learning how to be better Christians.

After I left The Vexed Hillbilly, Sundays with Hoppy were relaxing. We'd make a big breakfast, serving the other in bed the first few years. In later years we'd make it side by side, then I'd cajole some sex. We'd watch football, maybe take a walk.

But this kind of Sunday where I gave myself the gift of yoga and my favorite breakfast, then fed my soul with the creative sisterhood of the storytelling group were the most fulfilled I'd ever felt, except motherhood. Nothing trumped time with my babies.

Man update:

The DJ sent a video telling me he was grateful for me yesterday.

The Liberal Marine sent two pictures from his trip to the Ozarks. He has been the one I've seen the most since I broke up with Cranky. Up until last week I had seen him every week, once a week for six weeks. He's an interesting, smart, kind person. I know he would be my person in a heartbeat but I'm not there.

The Mail Man invited me to a fire in his backyard but I had a class to go to.

Tantric Man has texted often but he's making up for hard anal sex.

The SoundMan is in the wings and was texting profusely last week. We had a happy hour set up for today but I hadn't heard from him so I texted an hour before. He apologized and asked for another day. I don't know if people don't put stuff on their calendars or what. It's annoying. But I was tired and fine with staying home.

I don't know. I feel a change coming, maybe. One where I just date myself. I'm getting annoyed with all of it. Then tomorrow I'll go talk to five new people on Tinder. I'll figure it out. At some point.

xoxoxo

I've been on and off Tinder now for a couple of months. I get tired of it and delete it. This has happened multiple times. One reason I go back to Tinder is simply because it has the reputation of being the dating app for people who aren't wanting a serious relationship. However, not everyone has gotten this memo.

There are many bios that state:

"Looking for LTR" (long-term relationship)

"Looking for the one to make me delete this app" (or some BS like that)

The worst one is: "Looking for my last first kiss." (Yuck)

It's Tinder folks. If you actually want to meet someone go find another app. Even Bumble or Hinge is more for the relationship folk, especially Hinge. It's even in their policies. I have a friend who was ready to get serious. She ponied up the dough for eharmony, met someone cool, and is in a serious relationship with them which will probably lead to marriage.

Besides being on Tinder the other problem, to me, is this whole "looking for the one" scenario. It seems like that would put pressure on things from the start. Is it so strange to just meet people and build a friendship with lightness and joy and no expectations for 'til death do us part? At least not until date three?

A woman I met at a conference told me about a widower who is on the dating apps and is so serious in his search for "the one." She keeps telling him to just relax and meet people. He likes hanging out with married women for friendships because then there's no pressure.

It seems like there are two larger dating philosophy camps of single men and one much smaller pool (well, and of course the married guys). The two larger groups are the "booty call-I want-to-fuck-you" guys and the "last first kiss" serious guys. Then there's a small pool of guys who have their shit together and say things like, "Friends first and see what happens," or "Take it slow and meet new people," etc.

I have five questions I ask potential dates and question five is the one where many guys decide I'm not for them. Question five is, "I'm not ready to be serious. I am dating more than one person right now. Can you deal with that?"Many can't. I just think the best man wo uld shine in a circumstance like that. The best man would cut through the bullshit and you'd end up spending more time with him eventually, if it's meant to be. I obviously would not care if he is dating others. That's cool. If you find "the one," go have a wonderful fun life my man. It just wasn't me right now. Is that a strange way to approach it? [46]

xoxoxo

---

46 A few years later I will learn how damn hard it is to be the one who wants to be monogamous and the man you kinda maybe fell in love with says he never wants to be monogamous. That story will be in *The Year of Abandon*.

Within a five minute span three of my favorite dates reached out to me. The way that they did so and what they were sharing made me happy. It makes me concerned that I'll never be able to be a one-man woman ever again because it is so fun to be a part of different lives.

The Brit is climbing into a racing car. He's been texting often the last few days. He is the opposite of most people, texting more during trips, and less in his normal life. Lest you think oh ho, he is married. I've been to his place. He's on the divorce train. He has been teasing me about the cardigan-wearing folk at my teacher conference. I have issued a challenge that I have a sexy cardi which defies all cardigan philosophy to take place at some point when I see him again. We have no dates set up. He texted me twenty minutes before climbing into the car. I got to watch online as he drove. Sexy as hell I tell ya.

The Liberal Marine sent me a song, nothing romantic or sexy. Just for fun. It's "Black Lung" by The Dead South. I've been worried about him as he has to put his dog down for biting someone. That's a soul-killer.

The DJ sent a photo of a game, saying I had no idea how nerdy or geeky his day was about to be. While not sexy like a race car, it is sexy to me that he is doing things that give him joy. He asked me out so we have a date next week. He's the only one on the docket right now. What I love so much about The DJ and The Brit is that they are living life to the fullest. They have passions and spend time doing them. The Liberal Marine does not. He is depressed I think. What I admire about him though is the way that he fights the good fight for rights for everyone everyday no matter how awkward it is. All three are liberal; a must have for me. I'm not interested in schooling my mate on politics. Nope. I've done that with all three of my serious relationships I've had. Not fun.

I see I've just said mate when I'm not looking for a mate. But I have changed my perspective a bit. It's okay to have some fun doing things other than just dinner and sex. I'm still dedicated to living on my own for a long time and getting to fully know who I am and what I actually want out of a partner.

xoxoxo

In a lucky turn of events, I snagged a spot presenting at the national English teacher conference in Baltimore. I packed a sexy bra along with my favorite cardigan, hoping I'd get to go from a "mild-mannered grammarian" to Superslut, from pedagogy to pet-a-boner[47] so to say.[48]

The minute the plane hit the tarmac I was swiping on Tinder. I matched with a ripped tattooed bartender who messaged immediately saying he'd just gotten back from a trip to South America. Muscles, tattoos, and travel, oh my. He invited me to come to the bar where he was working, then sweetened the deal with free drinks for my friends and me. We had other plans that night, but the next night I had dinner plans with two of the sweetest people who exist. I told the bartender I might make it and he put my name and three friends

---

47 I'm so sorry. I had to do that.

48 Utilizing a stereotype here as all the teachers I like to hang out with are National Writing Project teachers with none of them being "mild," including me.

140

down to get wristbands. They wanted BBQ [49] so we ubered to a place someone's man had told us to go to. We fell quiet in the car as the scenery went from hotels and museums to businesses with barbed wire around them. The driver pulled into a gentleman's club parking lot and cheerfully said, "Here you go!"

All three of our Midwest mouths fell open.

"Is the BBQ inside the club?" I managed to say.

He laughed and pointed to a tiny shack at the corner of the parking lot. Anyone who knows BBQ knows that those tiny shacks are the best but were we gonna lose our life or limbs for some good brisket? We asked the driver if we were safe. He said yes, as long as we didn't walk anywhere. We exited the vehicle, hustled our asses into the shack, ate some decent BBQ, then began to talk about our next stop. They had to leave for the airport at 5:30 a.m. so they were ready to head back, finish packing, and don their PJs. This would not do. I cajoled them into going for just one drink so I could meet the bartender. I told them I'd leave with them if I wasn't comfortable. I knew they were hoping I'd come back with them.

I'm thinking the bartender was making it sound special so I'd come because there was no guest list or wristbands. It was in fact, dead, dead, dead, as in we were the only three in the place. He immediately set us up with drinks and was a great conversationalist, asking us questions. My friends had their one drink. I wasn't ready to go back so they left. They weren't extremely happy about leaving me there but I assured them I would be careful.

He had tattoos on his fingers, the backs of his hands

---

49 Yes, we are from KC, BBQ capital, and these two wanted BBQ in Baltimore. I was just happy to hang with them no matter what food was planned.

to his arms all the way up on his neck. It was weird how comfortable I felt with him. The bar was still dead so we talked for an hour, then some people started coming in. When I came out of the restroom, he was in the hall and we kissed. He knew how to kiss, soft lips with a little tongue. He had to rush off a minute later when a bunch of people flooded the bar from a nearby concert. A woman a few decades younger than me was standing near my bar stool. As I scooched in, she apologized. She introduced me to all of her friends and then they just included me in their group. We headed to the dance floor where a 70-year-old grandmother showed us how to do a hip roll.

I noticed that one of the men in the group kept watching me. He was tall and kind of cute and the bartender was in the weeds. I might as well have fun while I was waiting for it to calm down. He was a longshoreman and showed me pictures of the shipments he'd handled that day which was kind of cute. I was having a blast talking and laughing with them. Then the longshoreman kissed me while we were on the dance floor. I began to wonder how this was all going to go down as I realized I had two men interested in taking me home that night.

The bartender had said I'd make a great poly. I wasn't sure about that long term but I sure was enjoying it in the short term. Because of this, I didn't think he was freaking out at seeing this other guy flirt with me.[50] Also he was very busy bartending.

Closing time arrived. The millennials wanted me to come with them, to get together with the longshoreman. The bartender and the longshoreman

---

50 I now know that just because you are poly doesn't mean you want to see your date kissing someone. There are as many ways to be poly as there are people in the world.

BOTH walked me outside, one on each side of me. It was funny, well to me anyway. The longshoreman wanted to be with me but also wanted to make sure I was safe. I kissed him goodbye. He and the millennials left, fairly disappointed in me.

The bartender got an Uber for me. I told him he didn't have to do that. We made out while waiting for the car to show up. He had a close shaven head, those tattoos, and these great biceps. The car pulled up, he opened the door for me. I got in, then turned to tell him goodbye to see him climbing in the car beside me. I had to tell him I had a roomie at the hotel and he couldn't come.

He laughed, waved goodbye and then texted that he read the situation wrong. I texted him he didn't, that I was totally into him but we had to share rooms. He said he knew it was unusual to go to someone's place on the first meeting but he'd have invited me. I was tired and drunk and just wanted to crash in my own bed. I got back and considered throwing up, but it passed and I got to bed about 2:45 a.m.

Needless to say, I woke up Sunday morning with a raging hangover. I had asked the Bartender what his Sunday schedule was, but he had plans with another woman so I was surprised when he texted the next morning asking about my plans. I was going to the American Visionary Art Museum then I had to head to the airport at 2. He messaged back that he'd changed his plans if I'd like to meet up at the museum and then have lunch. From our bit of kissing, the night before I was pretty sure that "lunch" would not involve food.

We wandered through the museum exclaiming over the oddities, then our hands and lips began to wander. When we'd find nooks or crannies, we began to explore each other's nooks and crannies, almost getting caught a few times. We walked outside. He pointed to another wing of the museum but I knew if we did that there'd be no time for a booty call, so I said we should grab an Uber to his place. He agreed. A heavy makeout session ensued right there by the street as we waited for the Uber. I could sense this energy from him that wanted to consume me. We kept our hands off each other in the Uber as we didn't want to hurt the poor driver's psyche with our horniness.

He lived in a hundred-year-old row house, on the top floor with two roommates. He had a sweet cat I petted while I gulped water as I was still hungover from the night before.

God though, once we got started. He kissed me passionately pulling my jaw and then tugged my hair. We kissed while removing our shirts and my bra. He licked and nibbled my nipples, then he pushed me onto the bed, pulled my jeans off, and went to town. He knew how to do this thing with his hand that sent me over the moon. Sex with the Bartender was very physical. Tantric Man had put his hand on my neck before but the Bartender squeezed harder. I was a little freaked out but just relaxed and it was fine. I definitely liked it when Tantric did it and might have liked it better had the Bartender been less of a stranger. I did think, oh I suppose I could die here, but then realized 50,000 people had seen us together including cameras at the art museum and three of my friends. He not only spanked me but slapped me around a bit, just in a sexy light way. In the moment I really liked it. I did get some great spanking and hair-pulling and sexy talk and he flipped me over. He's very strong. It wasn't a wham-bam-thank-you-ma'am but also not as long as other sessions with other people, which I'm cool with. I got where I wanted to be about ten minutes in and after that it was just pure fun for, hell I have no idea, maybe a half hour? We pillow-talked a bit but I had a plane to catch so we exchanged numbers and texted back and forth quite a bit today. After I got on the plane I noticed a sore spot on my jaw from him.

I don't want every encounter with everyone to be the same as that. I also adore slow, sweet love making, a quick wham-bam now and again is extremely exciting, and then this half hour session of very physical sex was fun. As I think back over the past few months I there were only two sessions I didn't enjoy, the stupid man who scratched my clit back in September[51] and then the anal sesh with Tantric Man. I'm testing my limits to see what I like and what I don't.

The Bartender texted later that he was bummed I didn't live in his city, that there was so much more fun to have. He said that was intro sex and, *There's far greater depths I'm sure we'd both like to explore.*

I asked what those might be. He said, *More spanking, Shibari bondage, electro play, anal, and more spanking. I like an ass that's a bright shade of pink and red.*

I told him anal was not a fave because of the soreness after. He said he didn't "go to town" on anal and that it was "ground shibari, light bondage."

I don't think I'm done with the Bartender. I think I'll make it back to his city at some point or we'll cross paths in another city. I'm glad I was open to the adventure. My two sweet friends were a miffed at me as I kind of forgot to tell them I was alive. Understandable. I think they've forgiven me now that they heard the whole story. Maybe.

xoxoxo

---

51 It was HUD #2, the guy I met when I broke up with Cranky.

"I hardly ever ejaculate," The DJ said. "I've trained myself not to."

I queried why.

"First a question, what happens when a man comes?" he asked.

"They make weird noises and faces?"

Somehow he didn't laugh at me, "Yes they do. But after that."

"They crash?"

"Yes, they 'crash.' They lose all their energy. I find that by controlling when I come I can keep my power. I'm on edge and it feels awesome. I come maybe twice a month, " he said.

He's smart as fuck so I should have known that this is a real, researched thing: seminal fluid retention. According to the Healthline website, seminal fluid retention can result in more confidence, less anxiety, greater vitality, and a stronger life force.

"That's super interesting," I said. "I'm the opposite. I feel more powerful and energetic the more sex I have and the more I come."

"I'm sure that's true for women," he said.

My way seems like a lot more fun. I guess this is one of the areas women might have a leg up so to say.

xoxoxo

I hadn't seen The DJ for 17 days. He was out of town, then I was. He asked me for a date my next free night. We went to a Thanksgiving dinner held by some of his friends, but first we had coffee and talked. We talked about various and sundry things. I felt formal and shy for some reason. He said something during coffee about fully being yourself and I got the sense he didn't think I was. I pointed at him and said, "You don't know me yet," and he said that wasn't what he meant.

We went to the dinner and I wasn't enjoying it, but I was trying my hardest. I know that the "we're friends as long as we're fucking" had really set me back and I think it set me back more than I thought, but we talked and kissed throughout the evening.

I talked to him after dinner about the as-long-as-we're-fucking thing. He said he knew he could have said it in a nicer way. I said I totally get that if we had someone beside us in bed we aren't going to call the other person. I explained that it hurt to read that.. He ended up saying he understood and said I could call him at 2:30 a.m. if needed, but I won't. I don't like to ask people for help and will not if I think they would not want that call. We kissed and it was nice. We went back to his place and did all the things. His place is super cool; he has this monster bed. We had sex twice, talked a bit, and slept a few hours. I left at 1:30 a.m. to go back to my place.

I was hurt over the friends thing. I guess I was thinking he'd be my friend forever, but we might not be lovers forever. It's perfectly within reason to not want that on his end. And it's perfectly within reason for it to bother me.

Sometimes I feel like I don't want to see anyone for a while. I just want to be home and write and read and go out with friends. Maybe I'm bored of dinner and sex. Maybe I want to be pursued. I realized I wanted two opposite things. Maybe I've had it with people right now because it's Thanksgiving which comes with so much family time that I need to be alone. That could be it.

I have to listen to my gut. I'm supposed to see The Brit Sunday. I may cancel. I see Liberal Marine again tomorrow; I haven't seen him in a few weeks. Tantric Man asked for every Thursday of December but I was busy one and held one back because I just wanted to. He says he doesn't know if he can wait to see me for ten days which was a sweet thing to say. I'm okay with ten days, maybe more. I will see how the next date goes.

Exhausted and cranky.

xoxoxo

Thanksgiving holiday is where we celebrate stealing our country from the Native Americans by stuffing ourselves with food at awkward family gatherings where many of us grit our teeth and listen to well-meaning advice from the family. My dad once again teased me several times about "all my men" and that I'm being too choosy and that I will be 80-years-old with gray hair and saggy boobs and be alone. Ha ha, he's such a card. So funny!

Dad also told me The Brit was a conqueror who wanted to conquer me. He didn't have to try too hard. I gave it right up. I didn't want to play some weird game where I pretend I don't want to have sex so someone will remain interested in me.

Why is it the hardest to be completely authentic to your family? How can I feel more myself in a bar in Baltimore with complete strangers than sitting in my parent's living room? Something was wrong with me I suppose.

I came home a day early so I could get some things done since I was out of town last weekend at the conference. Also I wanted to have some fun in my city. I was supposed to be on a date with The Liberal Marine tonight but he canceled. That's the third time. So I suppose three strikes and all. I'll kinda miss him. I think he's hiding from me because he's going into a drinking mode. I probably could have lined up another date but I'm gonna stay in by myself.

I'm considering a stint of no men. I just plugged "no sex" into Google and found an article that said you will fall apart if you stop having sex. Some of it has to do with your partner and intimacy so that part doesn't matter. The physical things that could happen though aren't great, like your vajayjay isn't happy if it isn't getting pulled around. It says that! Also having sex helps your memory and mine is terrible anyway so then where would I be? AND regular sex helps your immune system. It's winter bitches. I need all the help I can get cuz it's flu season.

Obviously I don't want to stop having sex.

xoxoxo

I went to Hoppy Sporty-Sport's house to get some of my Christmas decorations (he's still living in my dream house we bought together, an 80-year-old Tudor with arches and wood floors). I ended up helping him rake some leaves.

Every time I'm around him I poke at my feelings to see where I'm at. I don't want to be with him. I never have since I left, not even once. I have felt the melancholy and sadness of what I thought was going to be for us. I can still feel how much I loved him and still care for him. He's never once asked me to reconsider or made any kind of romantic move toward me. We hug hello and goodbye but it's very friend-like. I asked him if he was dating or had set up an account on a dating app. Not yet, he said, next year. I offered to help him with it, told him I don't want to see him on a date nor think about a woman being in "my" house but that I want him to be happy and would like to help. I told him he'd want to go on Hinge. Before I left I held his face in my hands and asked him if he was okay; he said he was. I told him he could call me and talk and that I cared about him.

The Brit and I are supposed to be on a date right now. He texted this morning at 6:30 a.m. to tell me he wasn't going to be able to meet today or going forward. He had reconnected with an old friend and they were going to give it a run together. I told him I hoped it would work out. He apologized for doing it via text but that I was "a fun, cute, great gal." I wasn't sure I wanted to keep seeing him so that worked out well.

Zen Man is a new match on Tinder. I'm going to go to dinner with him on Wednesday. He seems like a very positive person from his bio and our messages so far. We talked about getting rid of fear, him preparing his creek bank for some natural landscaping, that we are both ENFP. We'll see how that goes. Even though I haven't been extremely outgoing he has checked in with me several times over the last few weeks so I just asked him if he'd like to have dinner.

Scarlett in the den with a Festivus Pole

December 2019

The DJ and I made plans for Saturday night dinner and a salsa dance lesson. I said yes but then mentioned I had an important event the next morning. He said he was not responsible for me, but that he would be "fucking me to God." Hmmm... not responsible for me. No, he is not. I am responsible for me, so be responsible then damnit.

I texted back that since the event was important to me and I wanted to bring my A-game and that I "am responsible for me," I would be snoozing peacefully by myself by 12:30, for his "dancing and fucking planning purposes."

He thanked me. I asked later what he thought of it and he thought it was great. I dressed to the nines. I had this gold sexy ass dress that I hadn't worn anywhere yet. I was hoping his eyeballs would fall out. They did. We went out for sushi and talked and talked. He was quite dapper in a pocket square, scarf, and jacket combo.

Our most interesting conversation has to do with what he said a few weeks ago, that we'd be friends "as long as we were fucking." This is our third conversation about this. I brought up that he had told a complete stranger that they'd be friends, a male. He said yes, they might be. I said, but not me, not friends with me. He says he wants both, friends and sex with me. It felt very *When Harry Met Sally*, when Harry is saying that men and women can never be friends. Sally says they can. Harry says it's a lie, that all men want to fuck the women they like. It was exactly like that. I believe I asked if he thought men and women could not be friends. He says it's dishonest to do so. He says he will always want to have sex with me if we are around each other.

I did some quick research and this subject is still being written about. I find it a very neanderthal idea, that men and women can't be friends. There's some research and many articles on it. The most interesting one is from *Playboy*, which explores all the sides of the conundrum, pre-sex, post-sex, etc. I feel like this has to be a male-female difference. I fully believe I can be friends with a man and not have sex with him. Does this mean that my ex, Hoppy, wants to have sex with me? I don't think he does. He's never made any move like that nor have I felt that vibe. Now when I was at his house yesterday, did I think about it? Yes. I thought about what it might be like to kiss him, what he might do, what it might be like to have sex again. Did I act on it? No. Will I? No, I don't want that. I know it's not the best thing and I want to remain friends. It's important to me to be friends. I suppose I can agree that a man and a woman may think about that, yes probably think about it, but I think that putting that aside for a friendship is worth it. The DJ does not. It still makes me feel a bit weird, feeling that I'm not worthy enough as a friend. He says that is not what it means.

Still, it was a good conversation. I very much enjoyed all that we talked about.

We went to learn salsa and I was scared because I'm awkward. But it was fun! We did the lesson and then left to have time for some nookie at my place. We had time for great sex and some pillow talk and he headed out at midnight. He said he'd miss me as he's out of town next weekend.

xoxoxo

I bought a ticket for K. Flay, a female rocker I adore. I took a late nap so I'd be okay to go and then I was all tired and cranky and down and thinking of blowing it off. I was in my warm and cozy bed. Am I really going to walk four blocks in freezing air at 8:30 at night to go to a concert?

As I mulled this, I contacted Seester for moral support. She suggested I go for a few minutes and if I hated it I could leave. I went. I had felt so sad and blue but the minute I hit that sidewalk I felt better about everything. I got to the concert in time to hear one song from the opening act. I maneuvered and maneuvered up to the fifth row in front of the stage. Then someone moved and I was fourth. I stood there and danced and screamed. I'm proud of myself for listening to Seester and motivating my sad ass out of the warmth to go. It completely changed my outlook.

Something unusual went down. I've been to so many concerts since I left The Vexed Hillbilly including Tech N9ne, Slayer, Iron Maiden, and In This Moment, and never had people be rude to me. In fact quite the opposite. These girls who could have thrown me around, in their 20s, were loud and drunk. That's fine, have fun! However, they decided to move over behind me about halfway through the concert. They were shoving me and dancing on me. Not like normal stuff, this was very purposeful shoving me. This is not a mosh pit concert either. No one else was doing this. At first I tried to ignore them touching me. Then I turned and asked if they were trying to "be mean to me." God yes. That is what I asked.

I had to repeat it and they said, "No!" Then I said okay and touched one of their faces.

Then they still kept shoving.

I was looking around to see where I could go to escape, then I thought, "Nope, I'm not leaving this awesome spot. At least until I hear my favorite song." I have strong quads. I engaged those quads and then I pushed back, threw a little elbow. Pushed back more. And thought, "Okay here is where I get punched."

But no! They moved back a little and gave me my space the rest of the concert! This old woman stood her ground.

Two side notes:

I'm going to be more purposeful about making plans with FRIENDS. I miss my FRIENDS.

I realized today this is my first holiday season of my whole entire life to be alone. No wonder I was feeling bluesy today. I can own that. It makes sense.

xoxoxo

I was looking forward to the first date with Zen Man more than I have any other so far. We matched on Tinder a few weeks ago and he's been the perfect message-r in that he didn't blow up my phone but he stayed in contact and wasn't upset when I was so busy with my conference.

He initiated the contact each time. I like that. After Thanksgiving he got in touch and asked if I was back in a normal routine yet. I said I was and asked if he'd like to go to happy hour so we set the date.

Each time we messaged he was active doing different projects each time. I could sense this joie de vivre that seemed similar to mine. He sent a picture of the Festivus pole he was making. I could see his living room in the picture. The TV stand was circa 1960s, my favorite kind of furniture! I complimented it and he said his vision was to have mid-century modern in the living room and transition to modern modern as you moved through the house. That is some crazy kind of shit I would come up with.

He said he was thinking of putting together a Festivus dinner for the cool kids complete with airing of grievances and feats of strength, so then I told him my goal was to be seen as a "cool kid" and get an invite.

I chose SoT, a cute downtown bar that's just fucking adorable. He was a little late but let me know. I was fine to sip my old-fashioned and have a peaceful moment to myself. He arrived at 5:45 and we didn't stop talking until 10:45. Yes, the first date lasted five hours.

He talked so much, but his stories were funny. He worked alone and lived alone so he has a lot of words "stored up." He was cognizant of talking so much and apologized several times. Once he said he needed to get control of his ego, that it was part of talking so much, that he was "an attention whore." Even though he dominated the entire night's conversation he knew it and at one point he just stopped talking and looked at me sheepishly. It was pretty cute.

He'd even ask me a question and then when I was starting to answer he'd just start talking again. For a first date I could deal with it. I'm wondering if it's like a stopper you pull out and there's a big flood and then it will slow down. It's important to me to be heard and understood and I'm not sure how much of that happened. He said he had ADD and I can totally see that. But he was funny and kind. He has great friendships he's kept for years and years which I learned from the stories. He's fully knowledgeable that life has been very easy for him and that he's been handed opportunities and able to talk himself out of trouble.

He walked me to my car and I was glad that he kissed me. I'm old. Kiss me already if you are attracted. Let's get this show on the road!

They were good kisses. Very good.

He said I was definitely invited to the Festivus dinner.

I had to tell him that I had lied on Tinder about my age. I have 49 on there instead of 55. I noticed that when I turned 55 I was not getting any matches. I had aged out of people's matches. I don't look 55 nor act it so I don't feel bad about putting that age. I want to get it out of the way on the first date because honesty is important to me. I don't like lying about my age on the apps but I'm playing the game I suppose. I told him and he smiled and hugged me and told me I look amazing. He said it was awesome because I'd know things like who Bob Newhart was. I laughed so hard. He asked me out for this weekend. I said yes. We kissed a little more. His smile was so cute.

He texted later to say that he was sure it was hard to "fess up" but that he liked me better since we could discuss the 70s, the best decade in his opinion. So far I like who he is as a person. We'll see if he wants to know who I am more fully. And you know, the sex, if that part is good. Fingers crossed.

In other news…

I've deleted all apps except Tinder but my card has been hidden since Thanksgiving. I didn't want my hometown dudes to see me and have so much gossip; also I just didn't want to meet anyone from that area. I'm not in the mood to match with anyone new right now.

I'm feeling more settled or something and I want to work on other things in my life, not just meeting men. I've reached out to my girlfriends and have two holiday events that I'm so excited for. I have family coming in too.

I just am not feeling the pressure from myself to meet new people constantly. It may be because I have Tantric Man, The DJ, the Zen Man and even The Poet is still in contact. He's been texting and has extended two very last minute invitations to hang out but I've been busy already both times. As I said before, his millennial ass will have to chase me down. I'm open to seeing him again but after our snafu a few weeks ago I'm not worrying about it or making any moves toward him.

Oh, Liberal Marine reached out to tell me he has some health problems, which I had figured out about a month ago on our last date. He can't get too excited so he can't see me or talk about sex. He teased me that it's my fault because he was trying to keep up with me. I truly hope he will be okay. He's a good person through and through.

xoxoxo

Zen Man asked me out immediately after the first date for the weekend and I said I'd love to. He texted Friday asking what I'd like to do, that we could do whatever I wanted, go somewhere in the city or have cocktails at his place.

It's cuffing season and I felt like cuddling. And Zen Man is very cuddly so I said I'd like to come to his place. I offered to make Chicken Fettuccine Alfredo but he didn't want to "share me with the kitchen," which I thought was a sweet way to say he wanted to spend time with me. When I shared that with two friends, one a millennial and one a Gen X, they both wrinkled their noses. I find it interesting that when I share something I think is sweet, inevitably someone thinks it is weird. I'm a fan of sweet romantic texts but I think they think the texts are fake or manipulative or something. Each to his own I suppose.

I had a super busy day of yoga and a six-hour meeting and then happy hour with some friends, so I was tired but I rallied and took a quick shower, wore my vintage shirt which I thought he'd like since he's a mid-century buff. He asked me to bring old-fashioned makings, that he had the whiskey, so I brought bitters, oranges, and the big square ice cubes.

When I got there he showed me the house he is re-doing. He's doing it all himself which is sexy to me. His enthusiasm and energy for it are also. I made the drinks and we started watching *2001: A Space Odyssey*. I had never seen it and he is a FAN, as in he knows all the cool facts about it. We were sitting on the couch watching it, sipping our Old-Fashioneds, and he was telling me some things about it but not too much because he "didn't want to ruin it." We held hands.

I probably should have kissed him right when I walked in but I didn't and then I was going with the flow to see what would happen. We watched the movie, he ordered pizza and we held hands. He said after we "met HAL" we'd go listen to records if I wanted. I wanted. We moved to his circa 1972 den. It's still in progress but it has a great sound system, a mid-century couch and a fake fireplace. I felt like I was in high school. We were listening to records and talking and cuddling and I was wondering if he was ever going to kiss me again. We did this for an hour. It was nice.

I began touching his hair and he stood up and held out his hand and we slow danced and made out. From there we very slowly made our way to removing items of clothing, paying attention to each part. Every time a record would end he'd go flip it or put a new one. I didn't mind. I forgot to tell you that his obsession with Space Odyssey is eclipsed by his knowledge and fascination with music. He chose Billy Joel's "The Stranger" for booty time. We got to "She's Always A Woman To Me" when I was on top staring into his eyes.

The first time with anyone is a bit awkward and this was no different. I look forward to round two to see how it will go. I had considered spending the night but wanted to go home to my own bed.

I asked him if he'd like to come see my place and go to dinner on Sunday evening. He said he would. It was now 1:30 in the morning so it was early Sunday morning. Something he had mentioned to me was that women always wanted to be "friends" with him. He said it in a funny way and I thought of The DJ and how I'd said that to him sort of. As I left he said he'd look forward to seeing me but that if I changed my mind and wanted to be his friend or had something to do he'd be fine. He said he enjoyed his own company. I believe him but Cranky Pants used to say that so much at the beginning.

He had a best friend coming over to watch the football game. I checked the game time and it was going to be too late to meet tonight so I offered Monday. He's coming in then.

I was with people from 8 a.m. until 1:30 a.m. yesterday. I even had brunch with my daughter this morning but I'm feeling a bit lonely today. Honestly I'd kinda like to be cuddling on the couch with him. But I need to clean, do laundry, and some homework. I have a book talk with friends on Tuesday, a date with Tantric Man Thursday, and a dive bar crawl on Friday. Sundays have always been hard. If I have stuff planned all day I worry I won't be rested for Monday. But if I'm chill and by myself I'm sad and lonely.

What would a "perfect" Sunday be? Early morning sex with my lifetime partner, coffee and breakfast in bed reading the Sunday Times or watching *CBS Sunday morning*, then get out of the house depending on the season: bike, hike, kayak, museum, movie, read books at a coffee shop or park. Back home for a nap and sex. Dinner with friends sometimes, and sometimes just us.

Yeah. That's my goal.

I have not told him that I'm not exclusive. I'm going to talk to him tomorrow night about it. He has said he is deleting his Tinder. I said he didn't need to do that. He said he couldn't keep up with more than one woman. He says I'm great. We'll see what he thinks about the year of sluttery.

xoxoxo

I had some rules set up for myself to help keep me single but I've broken some with Zen Man already. I'm trying to figure this out:

- I want to be single (Not "beholden" to anyone, my own woman)
- and have sex (Yes I want sex, preferably 2-3 times a

week)

• with people I like, (Why would I do this with people I don't like?)

• and sometimes have fun dates with them,

• and let them know I'm dating other people (and of course they should date others),

• and yet be flirted with, have some romance, be chased (I'm not sure these can happen. Most of the men so far put me in a category of unavailable and don't do romantic.)

I've changed my mind about some of the former rules I set. I wasn't going to do anything fun with anyone. That's literally no fun.

I am setting up more time with friends and plan to possibly start a book club for women next year. I'm trying to workout more and know that I need to get used to being by myself. I've traveled by myself, loved time by myself in the past BUT it was when I was living with people. I only have 20 minutes of adult conversation in my work day and that's not enough for me personally.

So the rules I broke?

I've seen Zen Man four times in a week. That's why I had the rules in the first place, because I get in relationships so fast. I told him I'm moving in three years. He said he listened carefully to that and heard me. I also told him I'm playing the field but that I'm open to a relationship with someone in the future, and that I had a date that night. He said exactly what I thought I would say, let the best man win. If I'm meant to be with him, I will be. If I'm not, I'm not. I don't think he'll still be here in six months if I'm still dating others, (or maybe even three), but for now he knows. He doesn't love it but he understands, so he says. I encouraged him to stay on Tinder and also date others but he again said he was not organized enough to have two women.

I really do like him and he has listened better now that he's not as nervous but he doesn't have the curiosity about what I'm up to that I think is important. I think he is trying to prove himself maybe. I'm a great listener and ask him questions. I'm going to talk to him about it next time we hang out I think. Or not. Just see what happens. I guess the reason to talk about it is to see how he'd react to something like that.

The four dates were the first happy hour, the movie night at his place, dinner at my place and a book talk that I was going to anyway. I invited him last minute when he queried about coming over because he was in the neighborhood. He went, he listened, he said he learned and was grateful to have gone. It's only been a week. We'll take it slower and see what is going on in a month. It took a few weeks for Cranky to begin to show his true colors.

xoxoxo

The last time I saw Tantric Man I went with the flow too long and ended up having a sore bumholio for a full 24 hours. He has made up to me with apologies and sweet texts the last three weeks. He asked for every Thursday in December but I've only given him one. I honestly couldn't do one of them and the other I'm supposed to go out with a girlfriend who will most likely cancel on me at the last minute, as usual. I'd choose hanging out with a girlfriend over any dude at this point in time because it is so much more fun.

As usual he was going to be here at five, then he texts that a meeting has run late and he'll be 15 minutes late. Then he's 15 minutes later than even that. Now I know the actual time will be 30 minutes after the time he says. I'm ready anyway just in case.

As always, he picks me up in his very nice sports car and we go to Brown & Loe, drink Luponic Ale and Framboise and split the meatloaf and mashed potatoes. We talk during dinner, he more than me but he listens closely and has great thoughts when I do talk. He has a partner and is poly so that makes things so easy for us with no relationship to worry about.

We then headed to my place for sex. There's no preliminaries whatsoever; he jumps right into penetration. Somehow this works for us. I don't know why. Then we have sex for over an hour, close to two sometimes, and it's crazy good. I always get leg cramps. He laughs. He's in amazing shape; the best physical shape of anyone I've been with actually. I had to change the sheets after he left, so a good time was had by me.

xoxoxo

I've hung out with Zen Man the most out of anyone since Cranky last summer. I like him but I don't want to feel trapped. I said again today I want to take it slow and I'm going to date other people. I told him how Cranky pressured me within two weeks to only date him. Zen responded with understanding and respect.

We went to see the Chiefs play and it was a blast. He didn't get all bunged up about missing the kickoff (maybe because he came up and we had sex before we left). I would have been fine to be ready for kickoff but he wasn't concerned. He said he DVR'ed the game and would watch it closely later, that going to the game was a social thing.

I went to the restroom while he was in line for boozy hot chocolates. When I came back I was looking for him. I thought this one person was him but that man was in a close chat with a young blonde so I was staring then I said sorry when she looked up. Then I realized it was him. We are pure extroverts. If you leave me in a line I'm going to be chatting it up with whoever is in front or behind me. She quickly showed me her boyfriend behind her and Zen made sure I knew they were just chatting but I wasn't concerned. If someone wants to be with the 24-year-old blonde they shouldn't be chasing me. I waved their concerns off and talked with her. She was all dewy and so pretty. He said later that his ex would have been so pissed.

He's been a better listener but I've also been saying, let me finish this story. He apologizes for interrupting and asks what I was saying. He says he will calm down the longer we hang out.

Sex is fun and we are having a grand time. We did it twice today, before the game and after. He said he feels like a young man again. He's two years younger than I am, i.e. one of the older men I've dated.

xoxoxo

I'm beginning to realize this ain't gonna be easy or simple. It's a mess, like life. I think cuffing season, my classes being on winter break, the fact that The Liberal Marine has been ill, and The DJ was traveling, formed a perfect storm of seeing Zen Man seven times in our first two weeks of meeting. It just happened that way.

I feel like I'm in the pattern of spending so much time with him logically to find out "what's wrong with him" so I can move on, but allowing the heart to feel too quickly. It feels a little like when I met Cranky and Hoppy and hung out so much right off the bat, my two relationships since my divorce. I'm seeing things I like but I'm "setting aside" who I am quite a bit just to see who he is. I have been opening up more in the last few dates though.

He said today something about "free love" and those type of people. I told him I am going out with a poly man. While I've fully explained what I'm doing, I just haven't said slut.

I was driving out to his place last night and I was cranky as fuck. It was cold and snowy and I brought food with me. I liked none of those things but I did want to stay the night at his place to just check it out. It wasn't great. Sex was just eh and he talked for four hours and then when he went to sleep he was moving around in his sleep so much I had to go to the couch. I actually thought about driving home at three a.m. but knew how upset he'd be when he woke up. I finally fall asleep on the couch.

The reasons I'm still seeing him: the core of who he is is a joyful, funky, rebellious, open, caring person. Today we had a long discussion about his thoughts after I told him I'm dating others and will continue to do so for quite awhile. He says he is going for the brass ring, that he may not get it but he's going for it. He says he knows if he holds too tight I will be gone so in the wisdom of 38 Special he'll "hold on loosely but don't let go." He says he'd rather have some of my time than none. He also said if things don't work out, he'd like to be my friend. He loves spending time with me and would treasure my friendship. We talked about the friendship thing; he says he'd get another woman to fuck but wouldn't want to lose me as a friend because I'm great to talk to and hang out with.

On another note The DJ called yesterday and talked. He said I haven't been flirting with him on text and was asking where I'm at. He's been out of town and I haven't seen him since the sushi tango date two weeks ago. He has sent some wonderful texts in the last week; some truly romantic and sweet words. I told him how the not needing me to be his friend thing had set me back and I was not in the same place as before that. I told him how I jump to conclusions about people, always good ones, and had maybe done so with him. We've been out four times over the last seven weeks. We've also talked on the phone a few times. He is interested in a relationship I believe, serendipity as he says. He said friendship drives my loins. It drives my desire to be with people for sure.

I feel ambivalent about everyone right now, except my friends and family. Even myself.

xoxoxo

The Poet and I were to meet for drinks at Dott Boss, a bar near my loft. I ordered my favorite, the Old-Fashioned. As I waited I picked the bartender's brain on how to make their version. I have to buy Dirty Cherries.

The Poet arrived a half hour late. When he ordered a vodka Red Bull, I choked a little. He slept two hours last night, had a bunch of deadlines, and still kept the date. He drank two of those horrid drinks. He's two decades younger than me.

We walked the half a block to my place, looked around for a minute, then we started kissing. He's an excellent kisser. I showed him the new bra I had tormented him about last time but I told him I was not lighting the candles. He accepted the consequences for his bad behavior of not coming over last time. We took turns removing clothing. Mother of god he had muscles.

Oh my, oh my, it was very fun. Went straight for the

goal. Stopped a bit later because he wanted to "taste me." Yes please. He knew what he was doing. I mean. Really. He does.

I offered to give him a BJ and he turned it down. He said he wanted me to finish then he would. I did. Then he did. Unprecedented.

We cuddled and slept for maybe 15 minutes and woke up for round two. I hope we get to hang out again.

xoxoxo

I should have just stayed home by myself tonight. Why didn't I? I'm on some kind of crazy mission that I need a break from. I think. I know some people do sober January and I'm thinking of deleting Tinder and taking a man sabbatical. Especially after tonight with Zen.

He got here and I was ready to go have a drink and go to a concert. That was our plan. He was 30 minutes later than the plan anyway. I walked down and had my jacket on, ready to go. Nothing doing. He wanted to come up and talk. I made clear I wanted to head to the concert three times. Nope. He was adamant that we go upstairs and talk first. I gave in. We came upstairs and he shared some boring things he wanted to tell me. It was an hour before we left. I was over the concert at that point.

We went to eat. When I tried to tell a story, he interrupted. Then he tried to listen and held his mouth or hands. He couldn't listen and it was weird.

Not. Going. To. Work. Nope.

He smokes pot daily. Fine for him but not what I want in my life. Then the sex.

It fell apart. The first time wasn't great. The second time was better and the next few times were good. I texted him he could shove me up against the wall and kiss me anytime he wanted. He said he could be that guy and turned into someone telling me to suck his dick. Then telling me exactly how to do it and how long, etc. etc.

Not. Going. To. Work. Nope.

I meant he could take me. He took it as I wanted to be dominated and told how to please him. Does it have to be that? I was ready for him to leave and realized he couldn't drive because he was drunk and high. His place is pretty far away. I guess I could have forced an Uber on him. I didn't. I gritted my teeth, like I do. At one point I asked him to leave. He said I'd feel better in a bit if he could hold me. He kept saying I'll leave after this album. The album ended. Finally I thought, I will have sex with him. It's ok. Then he'll go. That sounds terrible. I didn't mind to have sex. Would I prefer to be by myself? Yes.

I was enjoying it at first. Then it just went on and on and not in a good way. Then he was telling me to do this or that and I let him know I didn't love it. Then it was this weird conundrum where he needed to get off and couldn't and it had been several hours at that point. I gave a long, long BJ, and then a handjob, then a BJ again, maybe another hand job. I finally offered to use the vibrator in front of him while he worked on himself. I did my grin and bear it pattern instead of using my voice for what I really wanted. I said a couple of times what I really wanted and he would say just a few more minutes.

I am ashamed of myself. I let what he wanted come first, not only that I did things I didn't want to, at all. We are not in a relationship, a marriage or anything where I need to compromise and be this. Actually, I never want to be what I was tonight. It is too close to what I had to do with The Vexed Hillbilly for almost three decades.

The crazy thing is he is a really nice guy and I wonder if him being high and drunk was so much of it. I feel bad for him, but I don't want to see him again. But I feel like I should give him another chance. Why? Why am I like that?

The next morning I texted, *I just want you to know I'm processing last night. It wasn't good for me. When you left I was very upset and was not sure I wanted to see you again. I'm trying to think through stuff. I know you're an amazing person through and through. I do want to talk, just not right now. I've cried a couple of times this morning about it.*

He responded not to worry about Monday and to talk when I was ready and "you be you." Then later he said, *I know you're very conflicted. No matter how the conversation goes, I'm looking forward to it. My door will remain open to you.*

Monday was to be our Festivus celebration, the whole reason we went on the first date was that damn Festivus pole he had built.

xoxoxo

Zen Man has texted a few times and I haven't responded. I need to cut it off with him officially. I deleted Tinder and have zero interest in looking for new men.

I was glad to have a date with The DJ to look forward to. I got gussied up in a snakeskin dress that probably wasn't completely appropriate for a Monday lunch. I wanted to feel sexy. He texted that my chariot awaited. I walked down to see him nonchalantly leaning on his car looking suave and debonair, which I told him immediately.

I was a bit disappointed when his eyeballs didn't fall out at my dress. Still glad I dressed up for myself though. I'd never been to Lidia's, an Italian restaurant. It was gorgeous, the service was amazing, and we had the best bottle of wine I've ever had. I could drink wine every night if it were that good.

We talked about everything. I always have fun talking with The DJ. He mentioned, for the second time, that he wants a relationship. A few weeks ago he texted to ask if we were in a relationship. I said it depended on the definition of one. He said caring, respect, regard, and intimacy. I said then we are. We haven't had an actual full discussion on his thoughts on a relationship. That word scares me.

We made out by the car, and I invited him over for a booty call for Christmas Eve morning before I had to drive to my parents for Christmas. He said it would be more fun to wait and think about it. We hadn't been together for two weeks and two days. How much longer do we need to think about it? I said I disagreed but that was fine. If he had something to do, I'd rather he have said that, even if it was a date with someone else. The "waiting will make it better" sounded like bullshit to me. He dropped me off for my hair appointment and went on his way. After my appointment I went to a Christmas popup bar with Boo, whom I adore with all my heart. After a few drinks, I texted The Poet to see if he was available for a booty call the next morning. He was!

xoxoxo

The Poet
The Poet was so delectable. We didn't have as much time since I had to leave town. It was still so much fun. He felt bad that he came quicker than he wanted. I felt

170

happy he enjoyed himself so much he couldn't hold back. Sex with him feels normal and not strange like it did with Zen. His agenda is to make me feel good. There's this natural flow to it and we both have fun.

Before he left, he asked when I would be available again. We've talked about the fact that we are too different in age for a true romantic relationship, but that we are both busy professionals who enjoy having sex together. We are still figuring out what the friends part might entail. We have had some fun conversations about books and writing. I texted him later that I enjoyed it and he said my pleasure was his pleasure. Nice.

Cranky

I can't believe it... Cranky texted.

I broke up with Cranky the week of Labor Day. He didn't want to do the break-up discussion and sent me packing with, "I'm sure you have places to go and people to see," as I walked out of his place, fully bawling. I expected to never hear from him again.

Eva, one of my millennial girlfriends, recently said that men always reach out at some point. I said that Cranky had not. "He will," she stated confidently. I'll be damned.

The text came in on Christmas Eve morning while I was boning The Poet. It said: *Just wanted to wish you a very Merry Christmas. Hopefully you are enjoying time with your family.*

I had deleted his number so I sent back a generic, *Thank you! What are you doing for Christmas?* thinking it would help me figure out who it was.

Then I remembered I had his resume on my computer (twas in the trash) and saw it was him so I mentioned his daughter and going to his parents.

He said, *No, I'm here in town. Heading out on the 4th.*

I think he was hoping I was sad and alone enough to hang out with him. No and no. Later that night his friend texted me Merry Christmas with a bunch of happy faces with hearts. They must have been together, talking about me, after five months. I saw a meme that said, "Stay woke ladies. A Merry Christmas from an ex this week is the same as a 'u up' at 3 a.m. the rest of the year."

Liberal Marine

I had not seen The Liberal Marine since the first week of November, eight weeks ago. He got sick and told me he couldn't get excited so we couldn't see each other for a bit. We've still texted in a friendly nonsexual way though. The week before Christmas I asked when we would get to see each other again. He said soon he hoped.

On Christmas Eve I sent a photo. He didn't respond so I said if he was moving on that was cool, just to let me know. He said he had more medical appointments, and then, *As far as you, I just need a minute to get my health in the right spot and my heart. Not the black one in my chest, but the one I'm going to have to keep in check. I like you a lot.*

I responded, *That's wise. I like you too. Also though I know I'm not ready for anything really serious or even just one person yet. I always want to be completely honest with you.*

I get it. Me either, he said with a heart and a kiss emoji.

Goddamnit...Now I'm sick...

I had wanted to have a big week of a date everyday, but I'm sick and kinda pissed about it. I'm supposed to go to a New Year's Eve Eve party tonight and I'm not sure I'm gonna make it. Also I have no New Year's Eve plans.

The DJ had asked me several weeks ago. I said I thought I was going out with a girlfriend. He said he would craft a plan to pry me away from my girlfriend but then never got back with me. The girlfriend has not gotten back with me either. Boo is out of town as is Eva. At this point I'm home alone. I cried about it last night but I'm sick anyway so I need to just calm down. The reason it is a big deal to me is that as an adult I've had one fun NYE. That was at a concert with Hoppy in St, Louis. All the others have been depressing. I wanted to put on my gold dress and shake my big booty at a club with my friends. Not to be.

xoxoxox

Zen Man texted me off and on during Christmas week. He sent me a couple of songs: *Kansas City* by Wanda Jackson and *AM Radio* by Everclear. I did text him at the end of Christmas Day to tell him I hoped it was a good day.

His cat was missing, he said but a good day. Then he let me know the next day that the cat had wandered off, gotten a new bell with a collar as a present, and was taken to Animal Services where he got a home-cooked Christmas dinner. He sent a photo. It is cute. He also sent me a "happy song": *Where It's At* by Beck. I didn't respond.

A few days later he said, *I'm disrupting your life and need to step back. Let's be friends? We have gifts yet to be exchanged.*

Without even asking each other, we bought each other a gift on the same day. I didn't respond. All the family went home from Christmas and then I got sick and just didn't want to talk to him. I asked my sister what to do, telling her I didn't want to. She said I didn't have to but I should think about what I would want.

Well dammit I would want to know of course. That was the awful part of Prince A who stood me up and blocked me all in the same night.

I texted Zen Man all the things that had gone wrong with that last night and how I felt. Then I said I was sorry and I wished him the best in life.

He responded back that he was sorry and, *I was completely ignorant of your feelings and didn't at all get what you were trying to tell me. I was very self centered. I wish you the best too.*

Several hours later he texted, *Hey thanks for explaining what a bulldozer I was being. I'll work on that.*

I said, *I didn't want to hurt you but my sister said to do what I would want. I've been ghosted and hated it.*

He said, *Absolutely, this helps me. I hope it helps you too. :)*

I think I project what I want to see on men sometimes. Or I think I know them when I don't. I've got to slow my roll and just wait and see what they are. Don't put any projections out there.

xoxoxo

I'm sick. The only good thing about it is it gives me an excuse to be home and not feel like a big loser. If you choose to be home you are not a loser. Wait for a sneeze. God, that one hurt like a motherfucker.

I messaged The Poet and Tantric Man that I'm sick and we'd have to reschedule. The Poet was set up for New Year's Day and Tantric Man January 2nd.

The Poet was all que sara sara that's life baby. I was in a state of tears this morning from being so sick I didn't even feel like organizing my place. Also it's my third day of being sick, alone in this fucking loft and I'm over it already. Tantric Man sent a GIF of the blue monster from the movie giving the little girl a hug. I responded thank you and that I was pretty down and he offered to call and talk and cheer me up. I accepted and we talked for an hour. We had a great chat. I felt cheered. We were getting ready to say goodbye and my phone buzzed saying The DJ was calling. I told Tantric goodbye and called The DJ back.

"Hello Juliet!"

I was confused but laughing, "What are you doing?"

"Come look out your window!"

I saw him on the sidewalk in shorts on a 35 degree day no less. He asked if I was well enough for a drink. I would have had to be heaving vomit not to go. I threw on cute clothes, moisturizer and was ready in five. He didn't come just to see me but was moving out of his office nearby. So what? I was glad to see him.

He was in a black t-shirt and shorts and ball cap and this look works for him. I also like the whiskers he's got going right now. I've realized I really like whiskers or a well-trimmed beard. Very much.

We talked about family and relationships. I always, always like talking to him. I fucking love his eyes. I told him he'd dropped me for NYE and not "crafted a plan." He said he didn't want to craft something then I'd turn it down. He was waiting for me to ask him about it. I said I would never have done that. Twas a stalemate. He has plans tonight (I didn't ask what) and I don't.

But my sick ass needs to stay home and recover so I'm gonna work on some writing and do that organization stuff now that I feel like I'm not gonna die. Fingers crossed for next NYE.

xoxoxo

It's my first set of holidays in my adult life that I've been single. I'm a people person. I've been alone in my place for five days with one short foray out in the world on NYE in the afternoon with The DJ.

I talked to my sister for two hours on Monday night. My oldest texted me a little, but other than that it felt like the whole world had gone away and it was just me in this loft for with my sadness and sickness. I was so sick at some points I didn't even feel like watching TV. Part of the sadness was wanting someone to take care of me a little bit while I was sick (food and hugs especially) but mostly it was just being alone.

I used to love to be alone, when I was with a husband I didn't love and three kids I cherished, and then later when I was with a man I loved but wasn't extremely compatible with. I adored it, and looked forward to it. But now I'm alone so much. I'm a teacher so my job is with teenagers; there's approximately 20 minutes.

I adore doing things with people I like. However, I would rather be alone than with people I don't like. But I can teach 150 students all day, then do happy hour one night, a date the next, a friend the next, and love it. This has been a conundrum of being single. I want to do what I want when I want: eat, sleep, write, read, no TV, bathe, clean, etc. but I'd also like more companionship.

I miss the constant cuddles of my six-year guy but I don't miss how I made my life fit his. At this point in my life though I'll take some loneliness in exchange for complete freedom. I can see a day in the future where I will want that companion but it's a ways off, perhaps years? It would be super cool in a year or so to find another independent person who has a kickass life whom I enjoyed being around in all the ways you do and just start slow. It could happen. I think it will, when it's time.

Pussy Power

January 2020

I texted The DJ at 12:50 p.m. on New Year's Day that it would be fun to go somewhere warm for the weekend in a few weeks when I have Monday off, MLK Day. He didn't text back. I got nervous.

At 2:57 p.m. I texted, *Erm sorry. Just ignore the last text and carry on lol. No need to craft a reply.*

At 6:57 p.m. I texted, *Are you alive*

He: *Building my utopia.*

Building a utopia? What did that mean?

I text, *Sorry for the awkwardness above. The text was for you but then I felt ummmm shy? Scared? Idk*

He: *How you feeling*

Me: *I actually felt worse and spent most of the day in bed (loser). What will the utopia involve*

He: *Machines doing all the work for us and humans have all the food they need.*

Wtf again?

Three hours later I texted, *Ummmm okayyyy. I'm*

guessing you've been having some extracurricular fun, because he sounded high as fuck to me.

He called. He'd been playing board games from 11:30-9:30 p.m. with friends at his house. Strategic ones. I was embarrassed. He said he'd look for trips. It's been two days, not even a peep out of him. Nuttin. Not even hello or how are you.

xoxoxo

I deleted Tinder about a month ago and I haven't missed it. At all. But it was the end of the year, the holidays, and all the insanity of final projects for grad school. Also I have a trio of people I'm seeing: The Poet, The DJ, Tantric Man. I've been busy.

When I was down and out on New Year's night, I decided to download OKCupid and check it out, at midnight. By 10 a.m. the next morning, there were 87 likes. Four days later it's at 280. How exciting. I can't see these people though unless I pay $20 which I'm not going to do.

It has a tab called *Doubletake* of people "Recommended for Me." I'm not sure how they got these. I can swipe right or left like Tinder. If they've messaged me a little blue bar pops up and tells me. There are so many people it gets super tedious. I don't know why it feels more tedious than Tinder. If I swipe right and "Like" them and they swipe right and like me it supposedly shows up in Matches. I don't believe it because how do I have 280 likes and only 17 matches?

In the *Discovery* Tab you can search for age, location, and when they were last online. But then you have a choice of *Special Blend*, whatever the fuck that is, *Match %* which is the number of questions we answered the same, and *Last Online*. This is overwhelming so I just look at *Match %* but I don't know that I believe someone answering the same as me on those questions will make a good relationship.

Yeah I said that R word. I don't want to hang out with any dickheads, someone has to seem kinda cool. I mean I guess I've been kind of doing that but the change here is in my attitude. I had set this thing in my mind that I couldn't find someone cool because I'm not ready. I've realized what I'm not ready for and will never be ready for is being controlled. I'm not ready to give up my freedom. I'm not ready to have someone mad if I don't see them everyday. But that doesn't mean I'm not ready for just one kickass guy who has a life. I could be. Maybe. I realized I've been setting all these boundaries up for myself that were not necessary. Just relax. Listen to my female wisdom and stay open. I'm losing interest in OKCupid already, although I have four dates set up for Monday-Thursday, but two are The DJ and Tantric Man. Two are new guys from OKCupid.

Monday: The Hot Yogi

Monday afternoon I'm meeting a true Zen Master I believe, the Yogi we shall call him. Handsome as hell if his pix are true. He may be too intense for me. He's very into alternative stuff like yoga, philosophy and shiz like that.

He messaged me first which I like and was flirty which I also like, saying my photos were cute and he'd be happy to be more specific at some point. He was fun, flirty, intelligent and deep. We are meeting for a glass of wine tomorrow afternoon.

Tuesday: The DJ

Boo and I had a grand time last night, a tiki bar, then Bear Night (I can look you know), and then dancing at two places. I should have consumed water. I did not. It was rough today. I texted The DJ at 4:30, we were to meet at 5:30.

"I've been in bed all afternoon and I'm knocking back water like a bitch and I'm on the hangover struggle bus. I still want to come even though I'm not remotely at my best. If you want to see me not at my best-and possible alcohol-induced stomach upset."

He called immediately and teased me that it was a hard sell and his tone just sent me into laughing so hard. We moved the date to Tuesday and talked for over an hour on the phone. He has not mentioned the trip he said he would research after I asked if he wanted to go somewhere warm for my three-day weekend in January so that's probably not happening. But we talked and we talked deep, baby. We talked about past relationships, personal growth, and projects we are working on.

Wednesday: The "Why did I swipe right on him?" guy from the 'burbs

He has a nice smile and eyes. He's 52. His bio is kinda bland but that's okay. Everyone isn't a creative writer. I liked that he just finished up a degree and his golden rule is to treat the janitors like the CEO. I asked him for happy hour and he said he doesn't "drink and drive." Ummm okay. If someone has one drink and eats an appetizer and talks for an hour I don't consider that drinking and driving but he does so... the place I chose has drinks and coffee and tea so it's cool. I may not drink either as alcohol sounds nasty right now.

Thursday: Tantric Man
'Nuf said.

Prince-fucking A

Who do I see today on OKCupid? Prince A baby. His bio was an entire book about what he wanted. And didn't want. Listed in what he didn't want was FWB which he said he'd tried and it didn't work. When we went out he said he'd never tried it. It's me. I'm the FWB that didn't work.

I knew it. I knew he liked me and just ran away instead of having a conversation, instead of being a man and letting me know how much he liked me. He just cut and ran. I know he didn't want to get hurt. I had shared all of the year of sluttery with him and he saw my happiness at dating different people. I get that he didn't want to be with me, completely, and totally I get it.

But fuckin' man up and tell me that.

I sent a message on the app that said, *That is quite a book you've written in your bio darlin. Hope things are good with you. Good luck in your search.*

I can't see the message or do anything unless he messages me back, which I doubt he'll do. I am ashamed to say that I looked in my phone and still had his number. In a weak moment I texted, *Damn it to hell if I don't still think about you.* But don't worry. He didn't get it. CUZ I'M STILL BLOCKED. I'm crazy.

But…

I'd go out with him in a heartbeat.

Am I a dumb bitch or what…

xoxoxo

Five dates in four days. It was supposed to happen. Remember how I was sick last week? And I had to cancel everything? I wanted some D already and some male companionship, bitches. And some fun.

At this point I have 300+ likes on OKCupid but it's unwieldy. However, what I do love about it is that it has the most writers/thinkers I've seen on any site. The bios of some of these folk are incredible. They write a full-on treatise sometimes. I'm thinking that it's because OKCupid allows so many words. Three of the planned dates this week are new guys from OKCupid.

Monday: The Widower

This hot dude with some tattoos on his lovely biceps is sitting in a chair on a front porch smiling into the camera with his shirt on, no sunglasses. All the things.

We took it straight to text instead of messaging on the app.When he asked what I'm looking for, I said I resonate with what he said in his bio, which is along the lines of I'm open to what the universe brings but I'm not into being serious right now. He asked how much I've dated and said this will be his first date in two years.

He asks me if I can ride a bike, and cool me says bicycle? He says he has a Harley and invites me to go riding. On Monday. During work. I say rats I can't go. He asks what "rats" means. Okay that was a dumb thing to say but wouldn't the average 52-year-old American dude know what "rats" means? I begin to smell one.

I ask if he'd like to grab a slice of pizza that night and he says yes. I ask for a photo "right now" for security purposes and he sends one of him with a cute bulldog. His bio says he is 52 but he looks 38 so I bring that up and say it's fine, of course (Lord Jesus it is fine, he is fine), but just wondering. He says he will be 53 next July. I ask the name of the dog and a few hours later he says "Guapo" which means a handsome male. I ask if he's still up for pizza. Nothing. Two hours later I asked again. Nothing. I looked at the dating app and he had unmatched. I called his number just for the hell of it and left a nice voicemail saying I hoped he was okay. What was that? Is there a scam to get photos and my phone number? That's all he got. I don't think he was real. I just don't know what the point was.

Tuesday: The DJ

Tuesday I was tired as hell and asked him to come over instead of me going there. He said yes. Then later he mentioned seeing the Christmas lights from his place and that I hadn't done it. I said, "Noted."

He said I should just put my big girl pants on and come down. I said okay. He responded that he would make it worth my while and sent a reservation time for The Capital Grille, a fancy-dancy place I've never been to. Then the big girl pants things pissed me off so I chewed off his face through text ending with "Scarlett Jones always has her big girl pants on." He responded, "Noted." He's a card. Yes he is.

I went. I was exhausted and cranky and frazzled but I put on my gold cowboy boots and got my ass there on time bitches. And oh my. It was a good decision.

First off it was just good to see The DJ. I had to lay my head on his shoulder for a minute and just take a chill pill because I was just frazzled as all hell. I felt a little better. Then we got to the fancy-dancy restaurant and I felt even better as I drank some beautiful wine. We talked and talked. It's so easy to talk. And we listen to each other. Then... the food. Oh gracious the food. This steak for two was massive and we ate it all. Bitches, the asparagus and mashed potatoes were exquisite. It felt as if my body just opened up and said, "Oh we're being fed. Truly fed." I was a carnivorous beast just feasting. I needed that.

Then we went to his place and climbed up on his big

ass bed and fooled around for over an hour. He pleasured me with his mouth first, as a gentleman does. Then I must say I gave an epic BJ, possibly my best I've ever given, or the one I've gotten the most into. Some normal sex then he went to town with his hand and I lost it. Twice. We should have put a towel down. Ooops. I came home to sleep the best sleep I've had in weeks fueled by sex and wine and relaxation.

Wednesday: The Yogi
He is an intellectual. I am not. I'm smart but not an intellectual. I will probably annoy this fellow but we shall see. He's very tall and has a massive beard which he says might be to cover his face as he ages because he is having trouble with the whole aging thing. I'm ten years older than him but I didn't say anything about aging.

We went to a ramen place and had a wonderful conversation. It was fun getting a new perspective on life through his eyes. And he was a great listener. I felt out of my depth talking about some subjects. He knows all the names and philosophies and is just crazy smart.

I could see when the check was brought that it was a thing though and so I slid my card over when he wasn't looking. When the server took the ticket his whole demeanor changed to this joyful thing. I'm not wealthy but I just can't deal with the awkwardness of the check. I've never actually paid for a date's meal before. I've split with The Poet but everyone else has paid for me and I'm ever so grateful.

We talked for over an hour and it was lovely. Someone needed our table but we weren't really done with the date so we went outside. He gave me this great hug and kiss. Then we were making out, then we were kind of clutching onto each other. Yeah. On the sidewalk.

We considered heading to my place to seal the deal but I wasn't feeling it. We went for a walk and talked a bit more then I headed home. I hope to see him again. He's different than anyone I've ever met. But it's date one. I don't really know him, do I? We texted a bit this evening. It was okay. Not exceptional. We don't mesh, but he's interesting.

Thursday: Tantric Man

I canceled. I was so tired and had a headache. I am reading *Pussy: A Reclamation*. It is why I canceled. Pussy was not feeling it tonight. I honored her, canceled, and took a three hour nap.

xoxoxo

More Challenges (Since I already met most of those others)

1. **Learn how to hand my number to a sexy man in the proper way which means:**
   - Don't throw it at him and run away. (Trivia Man)
   - Don't hand him a business card and run away. (Guy at breakfast)
   - Flirt a little first (so scary to me.)
   - Talk after handing him the number? (OMG)
2. **Try a threesome.**
3. **Go to a singles group Meetup.**
4. **Go camping with a man** (Not a first date, duh, I don't want to be buried in the woods.)
5. **Go to a chair dance class.**
6. **Do the chair dance for a man.**
7. **Go to a strip club.**
8. **Go dancing at a swinger club** (Will need

sidekicks to do this).

9. **Go to a full length salsa class.** (with The DJ?)

10. **Try some bondage** (I'm the bound one, with someone I trust, of course.)

11. **Go to a speed dating night.**

xoxoxo

I keep thinking I'm gonna calm down on this dating thing and then I have a "free moment" (which really isn't free, I should be doing adulty things like DoorDash to earn more money or cleaning) and I schedule dates.

Monday: The Poet

I was very ready to see him again as he has been fun in bed and very chill with no drama. We are both busy people and don't text until we are trying to see each other.

He's not a great communicator over text. I missed a Sunday morning booty call because he didn't pull the trigger. He texted, "Wake up," at 9:30 a.m. I was still sleeping because I had stayed up so late the night before, not out shaking my booty, just reading and writing. When I saw it we had a convo where I made it clear I'd like him to come over but he was concerned about the roads. Oh well.

We got together on Monday instead. We made small talk for approximately three minutes then got busy. He is just a very attentive lover. He doesn't ask for anything. I'm not complaining. He loves to pleasure me with his tongue and does it well. In the past I could not relax and enjoy this. I worried about everything. Was I "normal," did everything look and erm… smell okay, etc. I take care to be ready for my dates and then I try to relax. I'm the most relaxed with him in this area for some reason. I think it's because he really likes it and is doing it because he wants to, not so I will reciprocate. In fact he hasn't wanted me to yet. Then when I can barely stand it anymore we have this luscious missionary-style sex, and it's just so good. I feel properly fucked and I also get to touch his head, biceps, back and butt during sex. It's very sensual.

Unfortunately the tongue portion perhaps lasted a bit too long which I didn't realize until 24 hours later. In the past I would have just dealt with it and been shy. Not now. I texted him last night, *While I wholly enjoyed it at the time, I'm feeling some discomfort in the clitoral region from the vociferousness of the oral part of our fun. Might need a bit less pressure.*

He sent a thumbs up.

Wednesday: The Yogi

I went on a first date with the Yogi last Wednesday. I thought about that passion on the sidewalk many times over the last week. I texted him Monday to see if he'd like to come over for wine and talk and kissing. He said he had a lot going on emotionally. I had no idea how to respond to that. It wasn't a no; it wasn't a yes.

I made a comment of some sort and then asked how I could help to which he replied I could do nothing, that people could not be rescued. I was at a loss again and just said I wasn't trying to rescue him and he said good. Gracious me. What to do with all that. That is too much.

I texted Tuesday and took back the invite although he probably wasn't coming. I said I needed to study and I did. I sent him my counselor's number and email because she is awesome. He said, *Practice good self care and try to relish the experience of your schedule. We can talk soon.*

That's cool. I will meet him again if he asks and I'm free, but I'm not asking again.

Friday: The DJ

We are going out for a luscious dinner. He said to wear cute shoes. We've talked on the phone quite a bit over the last few weeks. I called him last night in fact to talk through a bit of a family crisis and he was wonderful. As I had sensed when I first met him, he is a good friend, a great listener, has a wisdom of people, and someone who seems to really get who I am.

He has said that he can't be around me and not want sex so we won't be seeing each other if we aren't physical. My planner side gets in the way a bit because if someone is going to never speak to me again if we aren't having sex and if I don't want to drop everyone right now to just be with him then what are we? And does it even need to be defined? And perhaps will it change one way or the other? So many questions.

What I'm proceeding with is that right now we are good for each other, enjoying each other; tomorrow be hanged. There's nothing to stress about, I don't think.

The only other date so far is Tantric Man rescheduled for next Thursday. However I have two freelance articles, a journal, a quiz, a chapter to read, a show to write, and I really should do some movement, like yoga. I'm going to hang out with friends Sunday. Life is full. Possibly too full.

I deleted OkCupid. It was annoying. I didn't like that I swiped left on over 100 people on Monday. I sent probably ten introductions that weren't returned. We matched and I started a convo and they just were blah or didn't respond. I have too much going on to care about that right now. Also there's The DJ, Tantric Man and The Poet. I mean that's a lot for anyone.

xoxoxo

I had my first date with The Italian last night. We didn't text much but he did check in consistently to just say hello or ask how my day was this week. We planned to meet at John's Big Deck.

It's freezing cold but they have heaters and a plastic curtain around the deck to hold the heat in. I got there right on time and started chatting up another couple who was hanging out. I wasn't nervous to meet him, well a tiny smidge but really nothing.

He walked in and I went to shake his hand and then felt dumb, laughed and hugged him saying, "Why am I shaking your hand?" He laughed and said it was fine so we hugged then shook hands. We found a table and then decided to go up to the bar to order. He says things like, "Right on" and "yo." He ordered a beer and a Jameson shot. I've never hung out with someone who ordered a shot in the first five minutes. He was off the next day and I thought I would be since ice was coming so I joined him in a shot.

His favorite author was Stephen King and he could remember all the plot lines. I adore King but I can't do that. Even though I'm not much of a TV person, we talked about some shows I should watch. I made a list. We talked about our kids a bit and our past relationships. He was very admiring of how I looked and told me so with his words and his eyes. We got a little drunk and our body language was definitely warming up. He leaned over and laid a nice kiss on me.

I thought some food might be a good idea so we ordered and ate half of it. He went to the restroom and then I realized I needed to do that also. There was no one there but us and the bartender so I went down the stairs figuring I'd see him on the stairs. I did. He stopped and said I had to pay the "toll." This felt like a ninth grade thing to say but it was kinda cute too. I was gonna kiss his face anyway. I leaned over and we kissed. We kept our hands off each other but I sensed that we were both raring to change that. He dropped me off at my place and we kissed again.

I walked in and threw off pieces of clothing and lay down because I was slightly drunken, woke up at 2 a.m. with a rager of a headache, drank a quart of water, ate the rest of my sandwich and read until 5.

This morning he told me he was smitten and was going to flirt shamelessly with me all day. Then he told me how much he liked my eyes and smile. When he asked about my day I made sure to mention I had a date tonight so he knows I'm not just seeing him. We are hanging out again on Saturday night but he has an early Sunday so shouldn't be too late. He said he wanted to see me sooner rather than later.

xoxoxo

The DJ asked me out for Restaurant Week. It's still a bit icy so he texted and told me he was waiting in the lobby for me. He'd gotten an Uber and came in to walk me to the car. I felt sexy in my curve-hugging white "Marilyn Monroe" dress and my slouchy suede boots. It is so fun to dress up.

I didn't get to do that with Hoppy. He didn't enjoy dressing up or going out at night. How did I stay with him so long? Because I didn't know who the fuck I was really. Now I do. And I fucking love to get dressed up for an appreciative man and go to a goddamn luscious dinner and talk, then fuck our brains out. The DJ is always appreciative.

The Uber pulled up to the restaurant and he commanded me to stay put. He got out, went around to open my door, then had me hold his arm so I didn't fall on the icy street. When we were escorted to our table he pulled out my chair and took off my coat; he's done this every date. I feel queenly. Our hostess commented how gentlemanly it was. I think she fell a little bit in love with him.

The DJ looked over the wine list and chose a wine for us. This has been another interesting thing. This is the third over-the-top restaurant with wine and delectable food that we've experienced together. He chooses the wine and does the approving, then my glass is poured. I think that if I were the wine connoisseur instead of the man, the server would talk with me. But I'm not and I don't care to be. I just look forward to what is chosen. In the future if I learned about wine perhaps. But it seems The DJ and I have similar tastes in wine because every bottle has been perfect. I say all this because as someone who has had to take the lead in this type of thing if it were going to happen, it feels odd not to have to. Then I have to poke at my thoughts and feelings to see if I like what is happening. Then I do like it, then I think about if it is okay that I like that. Yeah I'm kind of intense.

We looked over the menu and discussed the choices. We are both interested in living authentic honest lives and isn't that refreshing? We also talk about men's and women's roles as I am fascinated and trying to learn more about living fully in my female powers while he is working on living fully in his masculinity.

After dinner we went to have a drink at a bar and I tried to put his hands on my ass and he was quite gentlemanly and said not in public. He definitely put his hands there not an hour later at my place though.

I hate feeling expected to give blow jobs. It is such a turn-off. It came up in conversation because this is the kind of thing we talk about. He said I should feel that my body is a gift and not any sort of expectation to be met. At my place we kissed, he pleasured me, then grabbed the condom but I told him I wanted to pleasure him so I did. That moment where I decided what I wanted to do rather than be asked and feel I should do it or say no and feel bad about it made it so much more enjoyable for me. We had some crazy sex and then collapsed on each other, took a wee snooze, then talked for an hour before he left.

He always asks what my schedule is and honors it to a T. I don't know if I ever will want to live with someone again as it is so wonderful to do my thing however I want to do it. I need some cuddles sometimes but I get through the shittiness of it with phone calls or just staying busy. I want to fully become my own woman with my time, my money, and my emotions.

xoxoxo

I'm working on a Fringe show. I'm having lots of fun deciding what to do with it. It's not happening until summer but I like to plan ahead so I met with a graphic artist last week. He seemed to really like the idea of the show and took notes. When I said I would make the postcards if he could just create the logo he seemed crestfallen and offered to design everything pro bono to enter it in ad contests. I was on cloud nine. Until today.

He emailed that after reading the show he didn't think he was the right artist and that I needed a female. Of course I'd like a female. But what bummed me out was that I was excited I had a professional designer who wanted to make a kickass logo and marketing piece for me. I immediately worried that the content of my show made him not want to be a part of creating the logo and poster. I have a contact in the ad world who already sent me the name of a female designer but I'm broke and just trying to figure all this out.

The designer thing might not have hit me so hard if a friend yesterday hadn't said that I should have a safe sex talk in my show. When my writing group disagreed, she said I was sleeping around with so many men and it sounded irresponsible. I've thought maybe my outfit for my show should have a big S on it for Slut (Scarlet Letter fans will get this. Okay there are no Scarlet Letter fans but those who read it in school... or faked their way through it will understand the significance). No slut shaming here. Sluts unite!

I am feeling great about not being on a dating app. I'm working on that female pack and have over 60 members in a Meetup, with ten coming to a happy hour and eight to a book club.

I had three, no four, kickass dates last week: The Poet, The Italian, The DJ and The Poet again. I talked to Seester for three hours on the phone Saturday night, hung out with Boo, and talked to both daughters. I went to two yoga classes this week and lifted once. Life is good.

xoxoxo

The Poet texted Friday afternoon to ask about my Saturday plans. I told him I had a meeting at 11 and then a date in the evening. He said there was plenty of time for what he wanted before 11 if I was up for it. I was. We set a time for 9 a.m.

As expected, he showed up a half hour late. I decided what was the point of getting dressed so I just had a robe on. We talked for five whole minutes then began a hot make-out session. He says I'm a good kisser but I think he is. We are good together. We just kissed so slowly really enjoying the feeling of our lips on each other.

In the past I have offered him a BJ and he turned it down. This time I didn't ask. I knew he'd like it so I did it. I knelt down and removed his cute joggers and went to town on him. He verbally expressed his pleasure then pulled me up and pushed me down on the bed.

We had our beautiful missionary style sex and then he moved my leg and I asked if he wanted me to flip over. He seemed surprised (he doesn't know me very well yet does he?) but then he used his tongue on me. This man knows exactly what he is doing. He knows where to go and how to go and was less rough on me this time. Then he flipped me over and said the view was sexy from there and why hadn't we been doing this before? He moved to stand by the bed and told me to stay on the bed. He took me from behind, then we came at the same time. Well it was the third or so for me but the biggest.

A perfect Saturday morning booty call.

xoxoxo

I'm reading Regena Thomashauer's book *Pussy: A Reclamation*. It is life-changing for me. Seriously. Life-changing. I am learning to value my feminine instincts and follow them. To listen to my pussy. That's shocking isn't it? It sounds crazy. It's not.

I grew up in a male-dominated home. I never saw my mom go against my dad. Add into that being immersed in the philosophy of the Southern Baptist that permeates the Ozarks which includes the ideas that men are the leaders, women are to be submissive, and the idea that the last shall be first. The women who were valued were quiet servants.

If you want to turn off most men in the Midwest say something positive about feminism and they'll immediately think you want to kill them and take away their "rights." This is my world.

I have felt second class and questioned myself my whole life. I remember being in a college marketing class where the professor and half the class watched our verbal communication with our small group through a one-way glass. We were graded on how people listened to us. We were to grab the spotlight and attention. That was the style that was valued. I had been taught my whole life to listen; I didn't know how to do this. I remember the most handsome white guy in my group was the "winner" every single time. The professor didn't bother to teach us assertive verbal skills, just graded us.

I'm immersed in feedback from society: the idea that using intuition instead of pure logic is silly, that women can't think "straight," that we're full of drama, we're chameleons, can't trust 'em to follow through, etc.

I was in an unhappy marriage for over 25 years because that was valued, to stay through everything. It took extreme courage to buck the whole system and leave. Then I fell for Hoppy Sporty Sport, someone who was opposite of my ex-husband in so many ways but still let me know what he thought about my clothes, my proclivity to analyze life, my music, films, etc. I didn't walk away or put up a fight, just caved so he'd love me. He did, but not enough to get his T-count checked, not enough to not drink every night, and not enough to go to couple counseling with me when he "forgot" to propose. Why did I accept so little?

In all fairness he's a good and kind man, he did listen

to me, cuddled (when he wanted), paid for most of the bills and took me to all-inclusive resorts at Cancun and Jamaica (his favorite vacation, hey it was fucking amazing).

My first step to listening to my inner wisdom was with the couple counselor. When he didn't show up for our couple counseling, it gave me the chance to work on myself instead of us. I left him last April, thus beginning the Year of Sluttery.

I found *Women Who Run With the Wolves: Stories and Myths of the Wild Women Archetype* by Dr. Clarissa Pinkola Estes on a Take A Book, Leave A Book shelf at my loft and fell in love with this book. It was meant for me to find it. It was the second step in my learning to value my own wisdom. I told Cranky I didn't want to give him a key to my place because of this book's impact. That started the breakup process. I listened to the feeling that kicked at me when I said I would give him a key. It was hard but I did it.

Now *Pussy: A Reclamation* has taken me to another level of not only listening to the inner wisdom, but honoring her. I can't convey the wisdom of this 241-page book in a few paragraphs. READ it. Read *Women Who Run With the Wolves* also.

Here's an excerpt from Thomashauer's book *Pussy: A Reclamation*:

"Pussy is where your intuition lives-- sometimes known as your gut instinct or inner guidance. She integrates information from diverse sources including the hypothalamus, neocortex, conscious, unconscious, and peripheral nervous system. This is why, when our pussy is engaged, we make better choices. We can feel the right next step in any situation. Women whose pussies are turned on make better decisions and move powerfully through the world. Pussy is truly our higher power, our no-hold-barred truth-detector, our way-shower, our leader, our divine director. She is, quite literally, our GPS." (p. 36, Thomashauer.)

Here's how I've changed over the last few weeks from reading this book and listening to my pussy. (Yeah I'm gonna keep saying that. Isn't it funny how shocking that statement is? Consider it.)

Sleep: I'm sleeping nude. I've never done this, never felt comfortable. Granted I'm single and sleeping on my own but I still had not done this yet until a few weeks ago. She wanted to be free of any restrictions. I listened. It feels so luscious.

Clothing: I went through my closet and got rid of all the stuff I don't feel gorgeous in. It was a huge tub. I kept them around because it was practical to keep clothes that fit and were professional. I didn't like them. Now I'm working on projecting who I am on the inside with my outside. For a meeting I steamed my new pink blazer that had resided unworn for a couple of months. There's a voice inside from my upbringing that says, "Who the fuck do you think you are?" when I step out of the box of the normal Midwestern women fashion choices. I'm ignoring it and listening to Pussy and what she wants. She wants me to feel good and show my joy through my clothes, shoes, hair and whatever makeup I decide I want.

At the thrift store last week I chose two things not on sale because I loved how I felt in them. At the register I received a 30% off to use that I didn't know I had. I was pulled into a vintage clothing store by her, Pussy that is, and bought a 1960s psychedelic gown, that's the only word for this thing. It's a goddamn floor-length gown with a queen chiffon attached cape thingy. I'm going to wear it to a Mardi Gras ball with a girlfriend.

Movement: I'm dancing more. I've always loved to

shake my ass but let "bad" dancing fall away as Hoppy didn't like my music and sort of mocked me for dancing. Now I put my booty music on and dance while I'm cooking. I missed it. I've started back to yoga as I adore it and it always makes me feel good.

Rest: I've canceled several dates that Pussy wasn't feeling and she was right every time. I needed rest. I was going to spend my precious time once to meet someone for the first time who I wasn't excited about at all just to meet someone new. Why? I listened to her and canceled.

Solitude: Staying home isn't being a loser. I'm enjoying my time at home on my own more. I'm writing so much and loving it. I'm reading more. I even watched a bit of TV. I'm still going out but when I'm home I am allowing myself to just enjoy my own company and not feel like this is going to end and I have to be constantly on the go.

Work: I have more confidence and have completely changed my communication style with men. A decision was made at work a few weeks ago that affected me without even the benefit of a conversation. I went immediately to a mentor and confirmed that it was ridiculous then walked straight to the decision-maker's office and asked if he'd made the decision. When he said yes, I told him in a flat voice that he'd need to change the decision, that was not how it worked. He acquiesced.

A male superior came to talk to me about another decision being made. I disagreed with the approach and said calmly straight-from-the-gut what I thought about it. I listened to his side and gave him a day to do what he needed. He didn't get it accomplished and I moved forward with what I thought was right the next day, emailing what was happening. He saw me in the hall the next day and said it was taken care of how I wanted.

I was denied the opportunity to go to a conference without an explanation. I wrote an email asking why and stating how it affected me and how it was a reflection of our organization. Within an hour I had a phone call from the second in command at my organization and received permission to go. That day the conference was booked and paid for. This is not normally how I operate. It's so goddamn empowering.

Touching myself: I've been forgoing the vibrator to learn how to touch myself properly. At 55 years old I'd say it's about goddamn time right? This is a direct result of the book. Thomashauer talks about the how and the why of stimulating your clitoris. I'm really enjoying this time with myself. It's not a second choice because a man isn't here. I could have a man here if I wanted. It's a choice to honor and engage pussy in a new way.

Have I convinced you to get this book?

Turn on babes.

xoxoxo

Pussy didn't want to see Tantric Man Thursday. She is done with him for some reason. Maybe been there, done that? Maybe she has better things going now with The DJ, The Poet, and the Italian so she doesn't need Tantric Man? I don't know.

I'm listening and canceled our date Thursday because I wasn't looking forward to it. I ended up going to dinner with The Italian. We laughed our asses off and drank some booze and made out. We have had two dates where we drank and made out and we've texted we were ready for more.

He came over for our third date. I showed him around my place which took about ten minutes. I had been wondering how the bedroom would go. You never know. It doesn't always mesh. I was a little nervous. We were making out and he said, "Shall we go to your bedroom?"

I gave a whole-hearted yes and led him by the hand. He was admiring of all the parts. Then we enjoyed the hell out of ourselves. He's solid, as in not thin at all. Something about him just turns Pussy on big time. It feels natural. I came like five times and he once; at the very end we were together. Gracious me. His knowledge of music, film, and TV is pretty insane. I told him he needs to be on a trivia team. He'd kill, as would The DJ, as would The Poet. Oh my god. That is the trivia fucking dream team. With me bringing up the rear to answer the odd question about Poe or beef cattle.

Sex went on a luscious hour; I kinda lost track of time. Then we went and stuffed burgers and fries in our faces at a bar a few blocks away. We laughed and talked the whole time. He's going to need to show a bit more curiosity about me and what I'm doing. Our conversations have been about music, TV shows he likes, family, film, and a bit of history, some politics, and a tiny bit of religion today.

I've been thinking more about Tantric Man. I think it's like this. I have two night classes, a full time job, extra duties at my work, writing, a book club I'm starting, yoga and the gym, a one-woman show to write, adult children, friends and then just the everyday stuff like groceries, bills, car maintenance, and cleaning that has to take place. I have a lot on my plate. And three men are plenty to keep up with. Tantric Man is the least fun of the four and the most expendable. He has a partner, he's kind of arrogant, his dates last 4 $1/2$ hours long and he can only meet on Thursdays when I'm usually exhausted from classes and the week. The DJ understands me the most and we have grand times together. The Poet is no drama sex on a weekend, and the Italian, so far, is just fun.

I'll most likely say goodbye to Tantric in the next few weeks. I want to wait a bit just to be sure. I met him last May so we have a bit of history.

xoxoxo

I was reading a blog post by Dating Dad, a letter to his future love, and thought I'd write my own. Even though I wasn't ready, it was nice to think he was out there somewhere.

Dear future man of my dreams,
Hi (smooch on your face),
I'm crazy about you. I like my independence but I look forward to seeing you and comparing how our day went, or our evening. We have our separate lives and our together lives and I'm glad you have a life outside of me.
I love hearing about your friends and activities you enjoy without me and I know you enjoy hearing about mine. Isn't it so fun? This is something I love about you. You are passionate about so many things and like me, kind of driven.

I adore your sense of humor, that twinkle in your eye when you're going to tease me or drop a bad joke. Speaking of that, I love your eyes. They are my very favorite thing about you because I can see all of who you are in them: your true compassion for people, your intelligence, your wry wit, your goddamn drop dead sexiness, your excitement for the people, places and things you enjoy, and most of all your love for me. Your ass ain't bad either but your eyes are my favorite and you do have nice calves, and hands, and the way your hair curls right there behind your ear.

I love that we can adventure together whether it's hiking and kayaking, or taking in the architecture in Chicago or New York or Siena. You have a curiosity that matches mine for authentic experiences and people and we have fun times together. Yes if we get lost we may get a bit cranky but we figure it out together and don't play the blame game. You like a good wander as much as I do.

I love our sexy times together, the passion and tenderness. You are an incredible kisser my man. Mmm mmm. I love holding your hand walking to our favorite coffee place to read near each other. I love laying my head on your shoulder at night and slow dancing with you anywhere we can.

I take so much joy from you and I can see that I give you joy also. Thank you for making me feel beautiful and cherished.

Thank you for being a man my children can lean on and for loving them as your own, as I do yours (if you have them). I love the father that you were and are and see that your children, and mine, have your heart.

Thank you for listening to me and even though you are always on my side, you show me another side if I need to see it. But sometimes you just listen and laugh, or let me cry on your shoulder.

Thanks for being a feminist and not rolling your eyes at that. It matters to you deeply. You share all the dirty work of having a home. Actually you are probably better at most of it than I am, but you don't make me feel bad about it.

Thanks for being healthy so I can have you around

another 40 years; yeah we'll be that cute 100-year-old couple on the news kissing and grabbing each other's butts. Alright. That's it. I guess. For now.

Winter is coming

February 2020

I did a thing. I downloaded Tinder again. I haven't heard from Tantric since I said Thursdays don't work for me and canceled last week. The DJ is AWOL on shenanigans. The Poet has been busy or sick. The Italian went out of town and stopped texting.

I matched with Smartass on Thursday and damned if he didn't make me laugh with his texts all afternoon and evening. We talked off and on for several hours and I asked him to meet me Friday night at John's Big Deck. As usual, he's not quite as handsome as his photos but he was still pretty cute. When I walked in, he turned to look at me, we both smiled then my heart did a little zingy thing. We drank and talked and flirted. I learned that he might want to retire to Florida, he didn't like to read, and he wants to be exclusive within a few weeks. All things that don't vibe with me. But I was needing some sexy time and he'd been a damn good kisser so I invited him over. When the ticket came, he griped about how much it was. If I'd not been so horny and the kisses not been so good, I'd have let him go just for that ick. When we got to the loft, he saw my book *Pussy: A Reclamation* and had no words; also my circus side-show photo gave him pause. In other words I don't think he'd ever appreciate the funkiness that is me.

However the sex…oh my. I rocked his world with a BJ he couldn't believe. He rocked mine too. Then we just fell asleep for an hour and it was nice. I told him I don't want to be exclusive. There was a definite downswing on the flirtiness the next day.

When I told him how I had to practice with my group at grad school by being a counselor and then a client he said "Hard nooooo" which tells me he's anti-therapy which means he isn't a fully formed man. But maybe I'll get to hit that D a few more times before he walks away.

xoxoxo

This has been my first football season to be single. I've watched games for the last six years with Hoppy. Before that I didn't watch much. I did other things and I didn't want to hang out with The Vexed Hillbilly anyway.

I spent several games at home doing homework or writing, just feeling sad to hear people cheering at a nearby bar. I did finally get the courage to go to a bar by myself and I've met Boo out at bars to watch the last few weeks of games. I didn't ask anyone if I could come watch with them but no one asked me to hang out either. My oldest says everyone has their traditions already set and they probably don't think I watch. I only watch the home team, the Chiefs. I don't care about any other team.

I've been sad over the season to be by myself or miss

some games. And unsure of what to do. I don't like to invite myself to join people as I feel like if they wanted me there they would've asked. Everyone knows I'm single and I'm newish to Kansas City.

Enter the Super Bowl. It's been an even bigger thing. I've cried about it two or three times. I know. Kind of crazy. But it's hard. No one invited me to hang.

I even reached out to two of my millennial friends to see if they were going out, a roundabout way of saying hey I don't have plans. One said no and didn't invite me. She's posted today and is home watching with her roommate. Okay thanks. Eva said she could come pre-game with me so we did. And it was nice. We went to John's Big Deck and had a drink and talked then she went to her mom's. I had three options at that point. The Smartass had invited me over on our date Friday. I was unsure about this as I'd just met him. A woman I just met today at my book club invited me over to her friend's house. Or I could watch at home.

I hit up the Smartass. He said it would be great. Then he said he had no food or alcohol. Okayyyy. That's a lie. Just say you aren't prepared to host me. I took him at his word and was figuring out food and beverage. It took an hour and several texts for him to finally admit he didn't want me there. He said he'd rather not have me come over as it had been 50 years since the Chiefs had been in a Super Bowl. Then why had he invited me and if he changed his mind I'd have rather he say so right off the bat instead of saying some BS about no food. Later he texted he was sorry for being wishy-washy. I unmatched on Tinder and am probably done with him.

I watched it at home by myself and it was okay.

I'm okay.

The Smartass messed up big time and I'm most

likely done with him. The Italian had mentioned it last week but has said nothing. The DJ is at the game. It's something to figure out by next season. I will.

When it was over I ran out into the streets to celebrate with my city so I had the best of all worlds, a drink before at a bar with Eva, wandering the streets to feel the excitement and then peacefulness. my own food and water and Tylenol for the headache I acquired from that bit of revelry. To be able to watch the celebration in the middle of it was a once in a lifetime experience. I even bought a Super Bowl champions shirt from a man on the sidewalk.

xoxoxo

I've read the Goodbye letter from Hoppy three times over the last year. The first time was the day I moved to the loft breaking off the six-year relationship with Hoppy. Four months later I read it again when I found it stuffed inside my suitcase where I'd shoved it on moving day. And tonight.

Tonight was the first time it made me cry. In all fairness I just watched "This Is Us," which always makes me cry. I'm sick again and so tired of that and finished with fucking goddamn cold winter. I'm jealous of all the people who have been in a warm place over the last month. I need sun and green.

I'm not on any dating apps. My only male communication this week was a couple of texts from The DJ. I felt disconnected as we haven't spoken for a few weeks.

Grad school is kind of eating me alive with a class where I spent eight hours on one assignment over the weekend. I called Boo crying in the middle of it wanting to quit my program. I realize I would have to take an F in the class as it is too late to drop. Unacceptable.

My job is tough but I'm giving it 110% everyday. Today was so hard in so many ways I can't write about. I'm a public school teacher. I feel that I've probably made a mistake in living with my heart and not my wallet. People say, "Your job pays in students' care. I'll never get a note from a kid." That's true. I adore my students, god I do. But the stress of money is constant. There is not one day that goes by that I don't worry about money multiple times a day, well I drop it at work and focus on students but before work and after.

I haven't taken my car to the shop because I like seeing $2000 in my savings. It just seems that there are the haves and the have-nots and it doesn't have anything to do with how hard you work or how much what you do matters. Welcome to 'Merica where it's all about business and law and medicine. Fuck you if you go into helping people, if you always chose people over building wealth, if you chose to leave your unhappy marriage and don't get to split expenses now, if you are there for your kids even if you don't have it and the ex just isn't. I feel it's shameful to be this way at age 55. I should have my financial shit together.

I thought I was crying about the note that Hoppy gave me, but I guess I'm crying about everything. Grad school, teaching, money, family, loneliness…

I'm crying about feeling alone. I've been alone so much the last two weeks.

I'm crying because goddamnit it will be my first Valentine's Day alone since I was 17 years old and how fucking stupid is that? I don't really care about it. It's so dumb. But I did text a girlfriend who's man lives far away to see what she's doing and she hasn't responded. I texted another friend earlier who also hasn't responded.

Sorry to be a downer but it wouldn't be real without these nights.

xoxoxo

"We are all filled with a longing for the wild. There are few culturally sanctioned antidotes for this yearning. We were taught to feel shame for such a desire. We grew our hair long and used it to hide our feelings. But the shadow of Wild Woman still lurks behind us during our days and in our nights. No matter where we are, the shadow that trots behind us is definitely four-footed." -Women Who Run with the Wolves- Clarissa Pinkola Estes, Ph.D.

Women Who Run with the Wolves meant so much to me over the last year. I read it from June to October, in between grad school and moving classrooms, getting involved with Cranky, breaking up, and coining the Year of Sluttery. I know I want it to be a foundation of my future work with women as a mental health counselor, a writer, and a speaker.

Estes writes, "...women's flagging vitality can be restored by extensive 'psychic-archeological' digs into the ruins of the female underworld." We are working to get to the natural state, the way we are to be, living our true wildish selves, listening to our inner wisdom, honoring the female intuition. The book *Pussy: A Reclamation*, by Regena Thomashaeur, has a message that goes hand in hand, or hand on pussy.

Trust yourself. Dig deep and honor and listen to your female spirit. She has your best interests always more than anyone else. She knows things you can't even put in words. That's okay. Listen to that intuitive wisdom.

Estes writes of how we lose this, very easily in fact. It

209

is not promoted by society whatsoever. The male strength, the patriarchy is honored in our culture. The feminine is demeaned at every turn. What is used to call someone a coward? Pussy.

Shouldn't it be scrotum, as that is the most sensitive area? The pussy takes a pounding and is strong as fuck. Those damn scrotums are little babies, shrivel up at the cold, poor things.

Anyway... I'm not here to trash men. And scrotums. I adore men. And their dicks.

I'm here to learn to reclaim my wild feminine, my pussy wisdom. And encourage every female I come in contact with, however that is, to reconnect with her "alpha matrilineal being."

Estes has this list of ways we sense her, that badass wildish woman we are. It is through our senses, through taste, touch, smell. Getting away from technology and television into nature reconnects us with our true selves, our wild woman inside.

Estes mentions breast-feeding. I remember the sense of being so fulfilled at nursing my children. It was a connection I'd never had before in my life. Yes it hurt like a motherfucker the first few weeks. Even when it hurt it was such an incredible connection and miracle. To feed my child with my body. I now understand that was part of this, the strength and power of the female.

Perhaps you feel the wild inside you out in the woods, if you put your phone away, that is, if you notice the sun dappling through the branches, that weird knot on the tree you just passed...

Or the water... the way the sun glints on each little movement of the water, the sound of the waves lapping at the shore...

I have allowed the winter to take away nature. I've been a big baby about the cold. Bullshit. I need to bundle up and get out there, even 20 minutes is rejuvenation.

It can be music. This is one that helps me when I'm not in nature. Thomashauer writes of the joy of shaking your ass. It is a connection to the wild feminine. Although I cried my eyes out last night in pure stress, before that I had danced in the kitchen to "Praise You" by Fatboy Slim.

I connect with that wild feminine in a good deep kiss or great sex, touching.

Estes says that when we regain our connection to our wild feminine we want to keep her, that our lives fall in place, not because our troubles go away, not at all. But that in the middle of life happening we are listening to ourselves, our wisdom now, "They know instinctively when things must die and when things must live; they know to walk away, they know how to stay."

Fuck yes we do. We know all that, if we will listen.

Estes says it so well, "When women reassert their relationship with the wildish nature, they are gifted with a permanent and internal watcher, a knower, a visionary, an oracle, an inspiratrice, an intuitive, a maker, a creator, an inventor, and a listener who guides, suggests and urges vibrant life in the inner and outer worlds."

Estes explains that this isn't religion but is psychology, "a knowing of the soul." It is us fully reconnecting to what we truly are. Without this... well without this we feel we are empty, dry, unfulfilled, constantly striving but feeling bereft. She has an entire page dedicated to the feelings one has when the relationship with the wild feminine is disconnected.

I can see it is the reason I lost myself in trying to get Hoppy to love me so much. I was glowing the day I met him. I know this because I have a professional photo from that very day, my editor photo for a magazine. God I'm beautiful in it. He told me my skirt was "frumpy," not on our first date, but within a few weeks he said it. I wore some favorite boho-style sandals with multiple chains to his house for our first date. He mocked them and I got rid of them and the "frumpy" skirt. Is that his fault? No it isn't. It's mine. I did that. I should have taken my beautiful smile and the beginning of my new life, worn that cute skirt and crazy sandals and walked away.

I severed any initial tie I was making with my wildish feminine that I had begun when leaving my soul-killing marriage. It's what I've begun working on in this year of sluttery, connecting to that feminine wisdom inside me.

Estes ends the introduction with the idea that story is what can reconnect us, story gives us connection to the wild woman wisdom inside, "Let us sing her flesh back onto our bones. Shed any false coats we have been given. Don the true coat of powerful instinct and knowing. Infiltrate the psychic lands that once belonged to us. Unfurl the bandages, ready the medicine. Let us return now, wild women howling, laughing, singing up The One who loves us so."

xoxoxo

Was I going out so much so I didn't feel this aloneness? So I didn't have time to think about the icky stuff? Maybe.

Valentine's Day is a manufactured dumb day. I've had so many bad ones. The worst were with The Hillbilly, pretending everything was okay. I'm fine to be by myself at home. It's a horrible night to go out for dinner. It's crazy, cramped, expensive and not even the normal good food a restaurant serves. I truly don't care about that. I just realized the similarities in NYE this year and Valentine's Day. I'm home and sick, again.

The slate of men is mostly cleared, which I'm mulling. I expect them to reach out if they wish to see me. They aren't. There are several reasons for this I think, depending on the dude.

One kind of dude really did have fun and likes me a little too much on the first date. He foresees, truthfully so, me walking away from him. He is protecting himself. Another type of guy doesn't like a woman who won't be exclusive from minute one and so is uninterested. The third dude is an asshole I guess? He pretends to be on a date and is really just looking for a one-night hookup. I might not mind a one-night hookup. I just want honesty, so then I'm not wondering why I'm not being asked to hang out again. The last kind I think is lazy maybe? We have fun and go on a few dates. He is attentive and then he's just not. The Italian is an example of this. He really liked me. He was "smitten." We had three fun dates. He went out of town and fell off the face of the earth. I heard from him once but he did not ask for a date. Now if I thought there was any possibility of anything really good with these people I would reach out to them. There's not. Perhaps they know that too.

I've tired of the game of the dating apps: swipe left on 100 weirdos, swipe right on 10 sort of interesting men, match with several, talk with one who makes the time, meet, laugh and flirt, have a grand time, be honest about where I'm at in life, maybe have sex. With many, it ends here. Why go through that whole rigamarole again: swipe, match, message when they could just ask me out again? I don't know.

I think most men don't have courage. I think they are little chicken butts. I think I scare them.

Except The DJ. I don't scare him. He texted today and called for just a few minutes. It's been four weeks since we've gone out. That is such a weird feeling.

The Poet isn't scared but that's different. A true FWB situation there.

I'm looking forward to spring, to bike riding, to warmth, to exploring my city, travel, building a female tribe, maybe moving in with Boo. Lots of cool things are coming.

I think it's going to be The Year of Discovery, just in a different way than I thought maybe. Less about men and more about me.

More about activities and friends, nature, wanders, writing, reading, laughter.

I think.

We'll see.

You know how I change my mind about things.

I do know that right now the thought of a dating app makes me sick.

xoxoxo

I'm an extrovert. I'm happiest with a female friend with time to laugh and talk, to communicate and listen about life and all its insanity. That's my very favorite thing in the whole world.

I realized this morning that I have an unusual situation. I believe most introverts would die a little inside at my normal schedule. I give to students all day. I try to squeeze in a short conversation with the two people at work who share their lives with me a bit; we're talking maybe ten minutes at max. I have grad classes with a group of future counselors Tuesday and Wednesday evenings for two to three hours. I've been seeing The Poet about once a week the last few weeks. I got to hang out with Boo last week on a weeknight and on Saturday night with his friends for his birthday.

And yet... I've felt so alone. So what's missing? That close connection, that extended time in person with people who get you and have no other agenda than to be with you, give of their time and life, share themselves, and want you to do the same. I crave it.

I think that's it.

Life since the Sunday after Christmas has felt a bit like nails on a chalkboard. I'm grinning and bearing it. I've cried quite a bit.

I've been trying to figure out what's up.

For one thing not many people do what I'm doing. What I'm doing is being alone so very much, truly alone. Now before you say, "Honey, so many people do that."

No, they don't.

Let me explain.

I don't have a pet. I see why people do; a furry sweet friend takes the edge off of that loneliness. A dog, especially, means you walk it and bond with other dog owners. At the minimum, pet owners are not fully alone. There's a warm, breathing thing that gives affection and takes some care.

I don't come home and drink wine or any other alcoholic beverage to take the edge off. I don't enjoy drinking on my own. I'm not into pot or other substances.

I don't watch much tv, have watched more since I've been sick the last week and I hate it. It does not make me happy at all.

I don't have extra funds to go to concerts and movies and travel so I'm home.

I'm new to this city. I have an adult daughter here whom I love to pieces but we definitely are not sharing our lives. My other two children are in other cities.

I have never gone to church in this city, nor do I want to. I'm not going to throw myself into an extra job or a nonprofit because I must have time for studying and sleep to stay on top of my job as a teacher. I need eight hours to meet the challenges of showing 140 teenagers that I love them, they are worthy, and put your phone away and do your classwork already.

I've felt really out of pocket and I think it's partially because I was using the dating apps as a time-filler. That was my pet, my wine, my tv, my local connection, my group. Hours upon hours I've spent since Labor Day swiping, messaging, meeting, wondering what-the-fuck, swipe, message, meeting, WTF.

I'm not sorry I did that though. I've learned about myself and had fun. Truly, I have! I'm not done having fun at all. I'm just taking a pause, a breath.

Of all those dates I'm still seeing The DJ and the only one I miss is The Liberal Marine. He is an unusual fellow for sure. I could fall in love with him. Almost. Maybe but probably not. Absence makes the heart grow fonder and all…

All these people in my life who hear I'm sad or lonely and are like blah blah blah, just do this or that. Check yourself on that list above. Bet you haven't "been there." Bet you've got a furry friend or family or friends or money or chemicals. I'm not judging. (You know I like a good drink.) Do your thing. Just don't tell me to get it together and be like you.

Don't misunderstand me. I know I'm so very blessed. I'm sitting at my window in my cute goddamn loft looking at a homeless person across the street who's hungry, cold, and lonely. And yes I feel like a big baby piece of shit when I think of that.

And yes I know we all get to have problems.

But still. I'm healthy, my loved ones are healthy, except a couple. I have a job I adore. Come on, I went to yoga this morning and then had a tasty breakfast sammy. Life is good.

I know that.

I also know I've been staring into the abyss lately and it's unnerving.

Here's to fellow abyss-starers. Unite. Arm in arm. At least we won't be staring alone.

xoxoxo

I had two dates this week that were so different. First, a booty call with The Poet. There is barely any small talk when he gets there. We kiss and get to it. Then there is pillow talk after. I asked if he minded if I went to a reading of his and he made a negative face so I laughed and said okay.

I texted later in the weekend to tell him I wondered if he thought I meant as his date because I didn't mean that. He said no he didn't think that. Okie dokie then lol. I guess it would have made him uncomfortable.

Then The DJ took me on an epic Sunday soiree that started with him getting his first pedicure. It was very fun to watch him try not to laugh during the brushing part. We then had time to grab a drink at International Tap House. I don't love chains but this one did have my favorite Raspberry Lambic so I was appeased. I just love little home-owned places.

But dinner, oh this dinner. It was at Le Fou Frog, a tiny French restaurant. They still had their Valentine menu out and I got to bring a copy home because the writing in it is exquisitely funny. All the food was crafted to make people want to make love, with aphrodisiacs and then the words of the menu also. Once again The

DJ has taken me to a place and treated me to a dinner that is in my top five dinners of my life. I would say three of my top five are with The DJ, only rivaled by a couple of places in Rome a few years ago. I mean Rome, come on.

I was a bit shy to see him believe it or not. It had been four weeks. It feels so strange to me, to know him but not know him, not really. I don't know him like I normally would know someone after four months. He turned on the radio to listen to something important, but it felt so odd to sit quietly while he listened since I hadn't seen him for four weeks that I finally questioned it and he turned it off. I felt, for the first time with The DJ, ignored.

Things got a little better at the pedi but it wasn't what I remembered for how we connect through our words. I was thinking perhaps we'd run our course. At the bar I was a bit downtrodden but then I mentioned I'd written right before he'd picked me up and he asked if he could read it. So he did. It was the "Aloneness" chapter. He said he felt it was the best thing I'd written, that I'm a differentiated person, not following the crowd, staying my course to be me. And he likes who that is, I can tell. And then everything was like how it normally was with him.

Click. I felt seen. That continued throughout the rest of the evening through dinner and then coming back to my place for sexy times.

At one point, I was giving him my look that I give when I'm trying to see inside someone's soul. I only do it to those very close to me; my kids make fun of it. It is unnerving. I just focus all my eyeballs and attention on someone intently. Kinda weird I know. He did a little kind of eyebrow raise at me, like what the fuck and I just laughed. I was staring into those eyes to sense him, just trying to get a full read on him.

I didn't get that read. Yet. What does that mean? I don't know. It's different with different people. He's a conundrum I'm trying to solve.

xoxoxo

I happened to notice that I had been paying for fucking Hinge for the last four months. For fuck sake, I haven't even been on it since October or something. Ugh. No wonder I'm broke. What an idiot.

I thought, well I don't want to waste the rest of this month and I'd like to have a date and I downloaded it. Well I don't have a date from it yet. I haven't been on it much and no one is being very fun yet. But what do you know, Cranky popped up.

He messaged on my photo of me smoking a cigar and said it would be more impressive if I were blowing a smoke ring.

Typical.

Dissing me but trying to be so funny about it. Yeah okayyyyyy.....

Then he said he missed my laugh and smile. I'm sure he does. I didn't respond to his Hinge message.

So he texted me.

He said he was disappointed not to get a response from his Hinge message and that he'd like to meet for lunch. He had a family thing to deal with but would be back in town Monday. He hoped all was well with me and that I would consider a lunch date.

I see no reason to go to lunch with him. I'm not going to date him again and we aren't friends, nor do I want to be friends. He wasn't even that great of a friend when I was dating him; why would he be a good friend minus dating? He wouldn't.

At first I crafted a message that is so typical of me, saying I was sorry for his family thing he was dealing with, making a joke, then I was going to segue into I was sorry but I wouldn't be going to lunch.

I deleted it before I sent it.

I sent a simple, I'm not interested in lunch. I'm sorry. I hope things go well with your parents.

It was hard.

I'm normally a person who tries to cushion the blow but I wanted him to understand that this was never going to happen. It's better that way isn't it? Put my big girl pants on and communicate. This is what I want from people and I don't get very often. I can take it. I mean, don't be cruel and evil but just straightforward please. So many men cannot do this. I must have it. I see why it is hard. But it's worth it. I'm worth it.

I have no dates set up and feel so ambivalent about all of it right now. I'm fairly sick of the average bullshit right now and not having it. I have some fun things planned with girlfriends Friday, Saturday, and Sunday. I may have a virtual date if a certain man comes through but I'm not holding my breath as the communication skills aren't great so far. I'm feeling healthier, have been sleeping better, and am almost recovered from being sick. I can sense that a better mood is around the corner. I think it is called Spring.

xoxoxo

After work I went to meet four new friends from the bookclub for happy hour and an event at the art museum that combined dance and photography. After it was over we had another drink.

We were all single ladies. One has just gotten on the dating apps two weeks ago and had her first meetup for tea this week. She said he was nice-looking but when he said he had to wash his hands if a dog licked him she knew it would not work. She adores animals and even fosters pets for a shelter. They didn't even exchange numbers. But she was glad she broke the ice. The other two ladies are not ready for dating right now..

We pulled the new-to-dating-apps lady's phone out and showed the non-daters Bumble. It was a hoot. We swiped left on three and she liked one man. She was disappointed that the message thing didn't show up so I told her how the app worked. We also fixed it so she got notifications.

I had so much fun.

I needed that.

Tomorrow is a writing camp thingy, then Mardi Gras Ball tomorrow night, a writing meeting Sunday and lunch with a college friend. This weekend is back to back to back filled with female friends, and creativity. Just what I needed.

xoxoxo

I matched with The Chef last May but then I started dating Cranky and didn't get a chance to actually go out. I liked his bio because he looked handsome and creative. I matched with him again in November. We talked enough at some point that I have his number in my phone.

In December, I was at the bar where he worked and the girlfriend I was supposed to meet had stood me up. I texted to see if he was there. He said he stopped working there recently, that it would have been nice to meet me, and perhaps our paths would cross again. Then we talked about going out the next night but he didn't text me back for 15 hours and I went out with someone else. All this had happened and we had never actually met nor really had an extended conversation.

Tonight he texted, *Hiya!* which I thought funny because we hadn't texted since before Christmas.

I said hello and he said, *Teeheehee whatcha up to?*

I thought this was really strange but had been really wanting some male attention so I said I was thinking about eating and asked what he was up to.

When he said, *thinking about making out with you,* I knew he had texted the wrong woman. I asked if he remembered who I was.

He said, *Shit.*

Wrong girl? Lol

He responded, *Hahaha.*

I said, *Lmao. Love it.* Then I sent a photo of me from the Mardi Gras ball last night and said, *I'm this girl.*

He said, *Cutie! Wanna make out? Lol.*

I said, *Maybe!*

To which he responded, *Well hell yeah then.*

You wanna come over

Ummm sure!

Lol. I love this whole conversation.

He did come over and we kissed in the hallway. Then we kissed in the kitchen. Then we just went straight on to the bedroom and it was luscious. I felt so comfortable with him. Let's just say I was vociferous in my enjoyment. He said he was trying to find the word for me which encompassed beautiful, funny, honest, and brave.

We talked a bit afterward. He's freaking funny as all hell and seems to be honest and kind. I asked if he thought I was crazy. He said he knew crazy and I wasn't crazy. He said from what he could tell I was creative and artsy, and had my shit together.

He said he didn't expect anything from me and he

didn't put relationships in a box. I told him that was perfect. He said he dated other people and always used protection which I loved to hear. He asked if he could see me again and I said yes. It was literally amazing, the whole experience.

A Pandemic Relationship

March 2020

I would have broken my don't spend the night rule except for one thing. My cootchie could not handle any more sex. We didn't have lube and were using olive oil. Well the first three times we didn't use anything. It was fun, but rough. We wouldn't have been able to keep our hands off each other if I'd stayed. How do I know that? Because we had sex five times in that seven hours. God yes we did.

We matched on Tinder. He looked so serious in his photos but his bio said happy hour or yoga so I said, *How about both?* I teased him that I'd show him how to do a downward dog to see if he'd pick up the sexual innuendo. He let it lie.

A few days later he said, *Are you pretty solid on the plan? I don't wanna go buy a yoga mat if you're gonna cancel.* I said I was solid and told him I was impressed with his ability to make plans. He asked if I'd be staying for dinner or "need to be out" which I thought was sweet. I said I didn't need to be out and he asked if I might want to be out then I told him he was a bit sassy and that I liked it.

I drove out to his place with my yoga mat, yoga pants, cute tank top with the sexy sports bra under my winter coat and a hoodie. I was a bit nervous but probably not as much as I should have been since our first date would be at his house and I'd be teaching him yoga. And a massage and dinner. He lived only 12 minutes from me. I liked all his choices of furniture and decor, that clean-lined mid-century stuff. He's redoing a couple of pieces.

I'd been there maybe five minutes and he stuck out his hand to shake mine which made me laugh. He made me laugh. Talking was natural and easy. I leaned over on him to show him some photos on my phone and he said it was nice. I showed him how to do some yoga and he was so sweet about it even though I didn't much know what the fuck I was doing. I had brought my book to help us though. He was adorable trying to do the poses. I moved him a couple of times. We were laying on our mats talking and I scootched closer to him. He grinned and said, "I see you are off your mat." I said, "So I am." Then we kissed. He is a great kisser. The best kind of kisser. Those lips.

I forgot to tell you that he's freaking hot as all hell. These gorgeous blue eyes, hair that is an actual style (he admitted to using hair products), great legs (perfect legs), thin but that bicep pops in different positions, an adorable gap between his teeth and a goddamn dimple in his chin. Shiza. He's seven years younger than me.

We kissed then kissed more, then I took my shirt off then he stopped and said something about being on the floor and I said let's go to your room. So we did. I told him I don't like anal. He didn't care about it. We had the best time. And again. And again. Then he cooked steak and broccoli and mushrooms, had cloth napkins and wanted napkin rings for them. Didn't want me to help cook, said he had it.

We talked the whole night and it was never awkward, never one more than the other. We began to sort of start staring at each other in awe at some point because it was obviously so great.

I may be in trouble here. He has kids, like young ones. Do I run away? I don't want to. But... this one, this one could hurt. I'm not walking away simply because of that. I like him too much already.

I forgot to mention he set up his goddamn massage table after dinner which was after sex which was after yoga and gave me the best massage. I mean he knows what he's doing. I was naked. He said he'd try to remain professional. I asked why? He didn't at the end. We had to head back to the bedroom. Hot I tell ya.

The olive oil got on his pillow case a little, nice new pillow cases (wince). The other negative after effect is that my pussy hasn't had this much action since Cranky Narcissist back in August and we always used buckets of lube to keep things going nicely. Like I said our first three times we didn't use anything and Pussy got a bit mangled. She had fun but she is in recovery, some serious recovery.

We both want to see each other today but we know we won't be able to keep our hands off each other so it's a conundrum because Pussy ain't having any action today, or tomorrow. She felt this way after The Poet a month or so ago and it took a few days. Worth it. Always worth it.

I'm in a bit of trouble here. He's funny, smart, and sexy. The sex is great with us, over the top as good as Cranky, better actually because The Masseuse can kiss (God can this guy kiss). Cranky would come at me with this open mouth like a cave and I'd try to capture it and make his lips come together. We are both "reformed" rebels meaning we have a bit of trouble-maker to us. We are both successful driven people who love what we do (he's in business, massage was a former life) and do it well but also leave it at work and have a life too. He loves his kids intensely and does the coolest shit with them. There were two painted birdhouses on his counter that he'd bought for them to have craft time while at his place. The week before they'd made tie-dye shirts. Seriously now. His childhood breaks my heart and that's all I'm gonna say about that. He's done so many things in his life, so many adventures. Damn I like him so very much already.

I know I know. Guard your heart. Be careful. Watch him. See who he is in six weeks. They can all pretend for six weeks. Yeah okay. All that. That is good shit to remember.

xoxoxo

Have you ever noticed how some people can consider your life outside their own and listen and even if they have zero interest in doing what you are doing themselves, they can appreciate what you are doing and be interested?

Then there are other people who immediately reflect your life on their own, their life decisions and they feel defensive and throw that at you. What to say to them? "Look darling I understand you have a husband and kids and adore your family life and cool for you. Why does me sleeping around offend you? I do not want your husband or anyone's for that matter. What does it have to do with you? Just go on your merry way and do your thing and I'll do mine."

More succinctly: "What I'm doing does not mean I think your life is not cool. I'm doing this for me, you do you."

I talk about my journey to people. Their eyes glaze over a bit and they look at me in horror, perhaps even a raised lip of disgust. Then they say something judgey. Why do people do this? How does what I'm doing reflect on you? I don't think it does... unless you feel "less than" yourself. It's not from me. The only thing I don't respect is not living your own truth. Even then sometimes people have reasons they are not ready to, and I respect that. Maybe they think sex is essentially "bad." I know times are a-changing in this area. There are people on dating apps who are "ethically non-monogamous," which is what I am, right now. (I think I will be monogamous again someday.) Many people I meet are fascinated, have a visceral reaction, and say something along the lines of, "I'm living through you!" I'm just still trying to work out how to have a voice and be assertive. I don't wish to be rude. I just want to calmly stick up for myself while not degrading anyone else's choices. It's a thing for me, knowing how to do this. Both of my girls can do it and I'm proud of that. That is from me, not their grandparents or their father, or their former church.

From me.

I guess I should consider myself and my voice as important as theirs then? Hmmm.... interesting.

xoxoxo

The Masseuse came over for the first time. I went out to meet him and walked him up to my place feeling nervous. It had been so great on our first date, was that real? We had face-timed twice the day after our first date, once in the bathtub! So fun.

When he got to my place he loved it and said it was cozy. We both wanted to jump each other but were sort of stepping around it. I finally asked if he wanted to eat or cuddle or talk. He said I should choose but I wouldn't, so he picked cuddle which ended up being crazy good sex. Then we actually cuddled up and had the best pillow talk.

I made dinner (it turned out perfect), salmon and asparagus and deviled eggs. I know most people have deviled eggs for picnics or holidays. I eat them year-round. He thought the deviled eggs were funny but ate four of them. He ate everything, even the skin on the salmon which he at first thought was icky then he tried it and it was crunchy goodness. We sat at the table and talked after dinner. I've not done that with a date but I usually don't have people over for dinner. I cleaned up the dishes a little and then we headed back to the bedroom. Then all of a sudden it had been four hours or more and he needed to go home.

I'm going to give this a go. After he left, I did several unprecedented things. I canceled a first date with a cute photographer. I texted The Poet and The DJ to let them know I was gonna give this thing with The Masseuse a solid try.

I hadn't seen The DJ in five weeks, twas Valentine's weekend and that wonderful French restaurant. I will miss him. We had fun. I told The DJ and offered to call and talk but he said, "I'm good dear. Very happy for you!" Then we had a short convo about current life situations and left it hanging.

The Poet had been checking in on me often over the last several weeks. I hadn't seen him in quite awhile either. First he wished me all the happiness then said he was really hoping to have me one more time before we called it quits and that we never expect the last time to be the last time. I told him it was very unexpected and could be long-term and that I had wanted to see him again and "if it crashes and burns" that he'd be my first text. He said, *We all deserve something sure and long term and fulfilling. Go. Be. Love. You ravishingly wolf-woman you.*

Then I deleted Tinder, not on hold, fully deleted. I had four matches that were still talking to me. I didn't tell them, just deleted it. I hope that's not asshole-ish.

I'm untethered. I haven't told The Hot Chef but he's been incommunicado. I'm thinking he will hit me up at some point and I'll tell him then. He may never and that's okay.

Why did I do all this after two dates? Because it seems like he really could be something serious (perhaps I'm wrong but no harm no foul). If not, I will be fine. I know I will be fine. I may get a broken heart but I will be fine. It's a good feeling. I am strong and good on my own but I'd like a companion, not to live with, not now, but someday. For now I'm going to get to know this guy and just see.

xoxoxo

He invited me over for dinner and I said yes. Then I got freaked out about COVID germs. Now granted this is not a crazy thing right now, not at all. I find it interesting to see the decisions people are making. Some people are still hanging out with family and friends. Some are holed up with a loved one or family. One person I talked to is making "conjugal visits" to women. One friend lives with an RN and posts nightly games and parties. I'm alone. Not even a pet.

We've been together twice already this week. He wants to see me. He's the only person I'm seeing, at all.

I live alone and go out to exercise once a day. I wash my hands vociferously after getting the mail or exercise or doing laundry. I feel amazing; I biked seven miles today.

Regardless of this, I didn't sleep and texted him the next morning that I wasn't coming to dinner so I didn't bring any germs to his house since his kids would be there the next day. He was upset. We both didn't communicate well the whole day. That evening I forced him to Face-Time me. He didn't want to talk. I told him that communication is the only way that this will work. He has this dry sense of humor that I will need to learn if this is gonna work. I said I like to talk things out. He said he didn't like to talk and thinks the "lamest shit ever." He's aware of his style and is kind of humorous about it. He's honest about how he feels and many people aren't.

He's got some trust issues I believe and I get that. I'm willing to give him some time to get to know me and see that I say what I mean and mean what I say. But if he can't see that in a few weeks, there's not much I can do. I can only be myself, say what I need, and listen to what he needs.

I think some might say it is bad to have an "issue" this early but I don't think so. I think we are older. We both have baggage. We both know what we want. We both are very enamored and hopeful. I'm not being a "yes" girl so that means talking will need to happen to understand each other. Also, let's be honest, a fucking pandemic adds an interesting twist to starting a relationship.

He's fairly adorable although he irons his jeans, a forgivable offense.

xoxoxo

I went to his house Sunday. We talked for a moment and then got busy. Our sexual compatibility is amazing. He enjoys my body and I do his. He has my heart already. I'm not telling him that.

We went to the grocery store to get food Sunday night. He made me laugh so hard twice that I did my fling-my-body-forward, hands-on-knees thing. We sat at his table, ate our grocery store sushi, and talked, comfortably, equally. We cuddled on the couch looking for a show to enjoy together; we like so many of the same things. He's a Mad Men fan for freak's sake. I saw Ozark and asked if he knew a new season had dropped. He turned and excitedly said, "Ohhhh, we could watch together!" We started it and it was nice sitting by him on the couch laying my head in his lap and holding his hand. He wanted to "give me one for the road" so we went back in the bedroom before I left.

Tonight he came over. I made turkey, fresh green beans, and fried sweet potatoes to surprise him. The sweet potatoes are a fave of mine and I was hoping he'd like them. He raved about them. Couldn't believe they were just cooked in olive oil with some salt thrown in. We moved to the couch after dinner and talked. I told him about W*omen Who Run With the Wolves.* He listened intently all the way through, making a few comments. When he saw how excited I got about it, he smiled. It made him happy to see me so happy. We talked about his kids and his work.

I'm open to seeing who and what and how and why he is. I know he could be a great person and I could love him but compatibility or some other issue could come up that is a no-go. I'll be okay if that happens. In fact this will not be an easy thing if he is The Guy. As I said he has young children; obviously would mess with my move to Seattle in three years. But with my new career idea of writing full-time, I can be wherever I want, whenever I want. I suppose it is something I really need to think about isn't it?

Damn it.

I actually adore having kids around sometimes. I think it could be okay. We could be in Seattle half the time and here half the time. It could work. I'm not walking away.

xoxoxo

It's only been two weeks. I've lost "cool" Scarlett, the one who deigns to be ignored or turned down. Okay I was turned down often lol, when they found out theirs wouldn't be the only penis visiting. That really bothers some guys huh? But now I've lost my cool chicky and I'm needing her back. But here's the thing, cool chick has a life. She hates being alone at home all the time. She likes to go and be and love, the ravishing wolf woman. I don't know if cool chicky can exist in this time right now, this apocalyptic pandemic world. This is pathetic crying girl who misses everything.

I asked a couple of questions about his office and his ex to see what cleaning measures were taken. And he didn't take it well. He said if I was concerned he understood and wanted to avoid visiting. But then quick as a flash he knew it was a "large issue" but was "tired" of the conversation and said goodnight. No conversation.

When I went to pick up my middle daughter from work at 10:30 p.m. she said to cut him a break that everything was stressful now, so I did. The next morning at 7:30 in the morning, he said he'd make the decision for me. We'd put off seeing each other until "this shit blows over." Was he mad I didn't respond to his goodnight? It was rude. I wasn't gonna respond to that.

I knew he didn't actually want to do that; he was trying to be a jerk. Perhaps he feels I'm yanking him back and forth but I'm not trying to. I read the news and consider and ask questions. I suppose it doesn't bode well that he doesn't take the questions well. It doesn't at all, does it?

I'm feeling so ambivalent right now.

Last night and a little bit today, I felt like I did back when I was 22 and I didn't know I was so smart and gorgeous. I fell for a guy and slept with him on a split in year three of my marriage. I fell for him and I lost myself. I remember he was crazy about me at first and chased me so I started looking at him. He dragged the line, then yanked and hooked me. Then he proceeded to ignore me. Sort of having an epiphany here. Do I fall for this cool guy thing? Am I still like some dumb fuck 15-year-old who wants the aloof guy? Is that it? Or is it that I can't conquer them so I'm enamored?

Fuck I don't know. But I'm feeling that right now.

He said the thing about not seeing each other Saturday morning at 7:23 a.m. and I didn't respond for two hours; perhaps that pissed him off. Then I said, *I know you are busy with kids. We'll talk tonight.*

He said, *Whatever.* Seriously? Whatever? Is he 13?

I said what the fuck and could he talk now. He said he was working on his bike.

I thought that meant yes, so I said, *So yes?*

Nothing.

Hey

He said he'd talk later around eight. We were originally supposed to have the whole weekend together, then his ex needed a break from the kids so he had them Friday night and Saturday. He said he'd take them home around two but was told it would be six by the ex.

Then he was gonna workout so that makes it eight.

I said I'd really like to talk soon then (wince), *I think I might love you honestly. I know that's so crazy this soon. I really need a few words but if you can't, should I take that as you can't be there for me right now?*

I told you I lost cool girl. She gone down the drain. Ughhhh I miss her. She's strong. This Scarlett this weekend was weak.

What does he say to this? He doesn't see the point in having a "stupid debate" about Covid and if I should come over. Then he said the issue is resolved.

I told him I never said I wasn't coming over. He asked then why do we keep having the same conversation? I didn't answer until five hours later when I asked him to let me know when he'd be home. He said he would. I said not to kill his legs on the bike ride as I was going to "fuck them off."

He said, *We'll see.*

I responded in a very mature manner, *Uggghhh seriously. IDK what you want from me.*

He said he wasn't in a particularly great mood. I said never mind. He said, *LOL sweet.* I called. He didn't answer.

I texted, *Answer.*

He said, *No I'm in the middle of leaving.*

I took a deep breath and decided to be the mature one. I texted, I didn't mean I only wanted to see you for sex which is probably the lame way you took that. I'm trying to be super patient with you. Really really trying. I took 'We will see' as you didn't want to see me which is why I wanted to talk and ask if that's what you meant. Be careful on your ride.

I went over. He said he wasn't good company and he wasn't. He said it was harder to pull himself out of the dumps lately. I took his face in my hands and kissed it. I hugged him. We talked about it. We should never text about hard things.

He made food. We got frisky and it was fun. We watched the second episode of Ozark and went to bed. In the morning he seemed better, in a better mood. He made me cheesy eggs and toast. He'd said he needed to go to Costco as his ex said they had toilet paper and wipes if you go before they open so we left at 9. I could have gone home but I was up for a Costco trip and wanted to see what it would be like in these crazy quarantine times.

There we were waiting in line for an hour before it opened, everyone standing six feet apart. It felt so weird. I got nervous which made me talk more. I was being my rowdy self and he said I was very extroverted or something like that. I asked if it was too much and annoying. He said it was not annoying but a "scoche" too much. I got quiet and sad immediately. He noticed. I gotta give him that; he noticed. And asked. I said I felt I'd been annoying; he said not annoying, again. He said he felt he needed to match me and that I'd want him to be more extroverted. Why would I? Two extroverts isn't as fun. I recovered and we shopped and it wasn't too bad. When we got back he remembered that he was supposed to go fix the treadmill for his ex. He felt bad he'd forgotten.

I had had this idea that we could spend the weekend together and it wasn't at all what I wanted.

She called and I was on the phone with my son. He gave me this look, I could see he didn't want her to hear me, so I went outside. I asked him about it. He said she knew he dated but why would he put it in her face because that would be mean. At first this bugged me but then I thought of Hoppy and how I'd do the same thing if I were talking to him.

Then he had to go. I had invited him over for pizza

when we got up that morning. I told him to wait and see how he felt.

I did my thing all afternoon and was getting hungry. I finally texted him I was starving and couldn't do one meal a day like him. He sent a kissy face. I had to ask if he was isolating or being social and that either was fine. He said isolation and he was sorry. I was tired too. I said no worries.

Here is what was not fine. One minute later he sent a photo of food he'd made. So he had been home long enough to make food and hadn't thought to tell me he wasn't coming over for pizza. I replied that I was getting ready to make some and that I was waiting to eat.

I'm sorry.

I said nothing to that. That felt to me how much he cared about my invitation to hang out, to be with me. It's understandable to need some time at home by yourself but it's not okay to not tell someone what's up.

An hour later he asked if I was all right.

I said, *Yes, you?* He was tired. But fine.

Six minutes later he said I was quiet and I told him I was writing. He said sorry, to ping him when I was done.

Is he a good guy? He said it shouldn't be this hard. Maybe it shouldn't? I'm trying to be me and speak up, build a foundation of communication and not fakeness. Is that bad? I'm not trying to reel him in; I'm just being me, messy, open, authentic.

A couple of times he has said I'm like the "others," who say in so many words, "I love you. You're perfect. Now change." It has made me so very angry both times. He says it when I'm trying to talk to him about something. When he said it today I grabbed my coat and keys to leave. He said was I not even going to talk? Just run? I stayed and talked.

I know that the current situation in the world makes this so weird. I'm isolated. I'm depending too much on him too fast. I'm freaking out about so many things right now and when I'm with him I can feel better, usually.

xoxoxo

The world is falling to pieces, literally, around my ears. Death, sickness, loneliness, anxiety, fear... it's a fucking shitty shitty time. As an empath I feel for everyone, my students, families with no jobs and all the worries, older people trying to stay well, it doesn't matter what your situation is it's fucking horrible right now (except the rich and famous, sorry I don't feel bad for you in your beach house with your pool and money). The news scares the ever-living hell out of me. The little girl inside me cringes at seeing people in masks. The videos of people fighting over toilet paper make me sick and disgusted. The empty shelves of necessities and anger at the hoarders. All of it. It's so much.

I'm an extrovert who's single with no pets in a little loft, a person who stays sane with people and nature. I don't have enough of either and am trying to make my peace with the idea that it's okay to just be fucking sad right now, to cry and sleep more and not be my optimal self. But there's a danger in that too. I know, for myself, that pursuing and chasing what I need and want gets me through. I can let myself have a pity party for a little while, but it's not going to help me in the long run.

I think I'm proceeding through the stages of grief with this pandemic. I was in denial the first week for sure, ohhh I can make breakfast and not have to get up at 5:30 a.m., cool! I can make my own schedule and exercise and eat right. I told my daughter I was gonna get hot. This isn't that bad! It will all be over in a few weeks. Yeahhhh...

Then last week I rapidly progressed through anger (this is fucking bullshit! fucking government) then depression, (several crying days last week and losing my own self as I wrote about) and then the bargaining (well if I can just have The Masseuse I can make it, remember going out with Boo, can I just have that now please, if only...) but I'm getting closer to acceptance.

I turned a corner last night somehow. I stepped back from The Masseuse situation. I was uploading so much pressure on that to be everything for me. That is such bullshit. I have to fucking grow up and take care of myself. I'm fairly ashamed.

This is it. I can't change it. This is the world now.

Get to it girl. What can you do to make it better for yourself and for others? Quit fucking whining.

Figure out shit that helps, like goddamn dance breaks. Another thing that helped was laughing my ass off at my adult children on a four-way video call. I had a phone conversation Saturday evening with a sweet person in my Storytelling group, an introvert. It felt like the first person who really understood how decimating being home alone was for me. She understood and communicated caring and asked how she could help. Unlike others who had tried to sweep it aside, "Yeah you're sad so go do a Zoom with friends. Go for a walk! Learn something new!" She validated me. Then she asked what she could do and I was ready. I asked to go hang out in her backyard when it's nice. She said I could anytime, even if she wasn't there. There's my nature hookup.

As for The Masseuse I'm stepping back. I'm regaining the person I want to be and am, strong, joyful, not letting dumb texts get to me. I can do this on my own without him. With him might be cool, we'll see. It might not. I'm concerned about his communication style. I told him last night I wasn't sure he still liked me, and I wasn't. He said he did. He texted 45 minutes later with an apology, *I'm sorry that I made you doubt I like you. I definitely like you... a lot.*

Hold on for a dance break...

The rest is still unwritten... I break tradition, sometimes my tries are outside the line... we've been conditioned to not make mistakes but I can't live that way. Staring at the blank page before you, open up the dirty window, let the sun illuminate the words that you could not find...

Yasss Natasha Bedingfield bitches. Go dance to it. Yesterday I danced to *Rack City Bitch* and the best kitchen dancing song ever, *Pony* by Ginuwine.

xoxoxo

In my phone right now texts all in a little row from the last few days: The Hot Chef, The Liberal Marine, Hoppy, and The DJ.

The Hot Chef texted Sunday evening. The opening volley was good, *DO NOT kill my sexy Fringe character.*

{Please God, will life be back to normal in late July? Not because of Fringe Fest but because I can't be a hermit that long. No one can! I'm supposed to have a one-woman Fringe show called *The Year of Sluttery* and The Hot Chef wants to come to it and wear a sign proclaiming that he is The Hot Chef.}

I said I wouldn't kill his character.

He was on fire with funny texts. He vollied with, *Sweet. Wanna make out?*

I said it was the best story ever, the "Wanna make-out" story.

He sent a pic of Shakespeare winking and then asked, *Is he fucking up yet?*

I didn't understand what he meant at all; in fact I thought he was high. He was asking if The Masseuse was fucking up yet. I thought he meant was Shakespeare fucking up.

At this point I'm still with that guy that I told you about. If it ends, I will hit you UP I thanked him again for making me laugh and he said you're welcome and that he was off to try and suck his own dick. Oh my.

The Liberal Marine texted me Monday. I haven't heard from him since January.

Are you surviving this apocalyptic bullshit

I said, *Isn't it awful? I'm surviving, yes. How are you doing?*

So far ok. As long as my job is considered essential I plan on plugging along I guess.

I asked. *How's your health? Take care of yourself. It's a mixed blessing to work out in the world now. Paycheck versus safety.*

He said, *I'm back at 100%. Most people with kids and families that are at high risk are staying home.*

Glad to hear from you and glad you are feeling good! Where are you working?

I was out for a run while this texting was going on. He was one mile from me. So I ran down there. I sent a photo of the building when I got there and told him to wave to me if that was it. It was. He actually came out and gave me a side hug and then went back in. It was odd, but sort of nice. I really liked him for a bit and missed him but I realized I'm over him when he came out. I want the best for him though.

The dream house Hoppy and I owned together is finally selling. I have to go this weekend and spend a bunch of hours packing up stuff I left there, which will suck.

The DJ asked me to be on his podcast. While we were waiting for the Zoom to start I told him he was looking hot. His tattoo was peeking out of his t-shirt where his bicep was stretching the sleeve. I always thought he looked hotter in his t-shirts than he did in a suit. Damn he is a likable fellow.

xoxoxo

Over the last two+ weeks I've dated The Masseuse, the most difficult moments have been when I was stressing out about COVID. He did not deal well with any of it, my concerns, my questions.

Well well well, guess who is finally realizing that this is a fucking big deal and it will affect lives and is stressing out. So much so that he canceled a date. He was supposed to come over tonight.

I texted him today that I was looking forward to seeing him. He texted that he was sorry but he was about to text me. He didn't feel like going anywhere. He thought he might be depressed. He said it certainly wasn't me. He wanted to ride his bike, go home, face-time his kids and just make dinner. It hit me like a slap in the face.

Two weeks ago he was upset with me for texting him I was not coming over because I was worried about COVID. Then today he literally does the same thing he was mad at me for. I am trying to figure out if he's playing me or if he's into his ex again (he says no, that he's concerned because she's the mother of his kids and it impacts them, which is totally true).

I told him I deserved an apology for how he has treated me over asking about it the last few weeks and he did apologize promptly.

He asked what I had going on tomorrow night. I said

I had an online class at 6 that could end at 7, (plenty of time for him to come over).

I said, *And.....*

He said, *And what....*

I said, *And are you asking to come over?*

He said something about it making a long night on a weeknight. So that's where we were? He isn't going to come over on a weeknight? I let it lie and didn't ask. I just stared at him and he smiled back.

I told him I was wondering if he was yanking me around, or if he didn't want to hang anymore but didn't want to say so. He said it was neither. That he was just stressed.

I said I hoped I could be someone he could feel stress relief with and he said he could but that he just didn't have the social skills tonight to "be bubbly." He doesn't have to be bubbly but I understand just feeling down. Also he is an introvert and is still going to work so he's around people and is talking all day.

I'm still in. I believe him. I like him.

I'm still maintaining my strong girl because nobody wants that other girl, not me and not him. I have my woman wisdom intact and am moving forward cautiously optimistic knowing that we are several steps back from where we were last Wednesday but that we could move forward again. Maybe. Maybe not. Not ready to walk away yet.

xoxoxo

I had thought The Masseuse and I would weather the storm together, his words. I haven't seen him since Sunday after fucking Costco. I'm being good and seeing no one. I did spend a few precious hours with Boo this week. It feels like throwing one spade of dirt into a big hollow well. He was the only human I was around. Facetiming doesn't count, although it helps a little, like a tablespoon of dirt into that well of sadness.

I just keep thinking how the tables turned. The Masseuse wanted to see me so much at first then this week he just wasn't there. I know sacrifices aren't made for brand-new situations. I know the mental health of he and his ex take precedence right now. I know I'm a big girl who can live in reality. I just want to make sure I know what the reality is.

I mean at minimum my goal was sex twice a week WHEN I WAS SINGLE. Forget about being in a relationship and not having that.

And yet... times are fucking apocalyptic. Weird shit is life now. Sacrifices are being made, properly so. If that is the reality I can live with that. If he pines to be with me but we don't see each other because COVID, because FAMILY, I get that.

I'm just trying to figure it out right now.

And let's be honest. It may just be enough stress to kill a new relationship, one that perhaps could have made it in the regular world.

I feel sad. I'm also trying to figure out how much sad is from the situation with The Masseuse and how much sad is from this whole thing.

I think I'm gonna just be a sad sack of shit until this is over. I kind of had a tiny grip on it this week and it slid out of my hands Friday. It's the weekend. It's a holiday. That didn't help at all. It feels better to me right now for it to be the week so I don't have this weekend idea. And hopes to see him. And wondering if he will cancel. And wishing he would be all over it asking me to spend all the minutes he has free. That's needy girl talking again. She can't help but be here a little bit folks because she thrives on people. I will try to be a mature, loving, understanding person even though the five-year-old in me is stamping her feet for some attention.

xoxoxo

The Chef texted, *Just in case nobody has told you today...*

Yes Chef?

You have an amazing ass and your titties are on point. Cute too.

No one has told me that today and I was really needing that right now. Thank you.

You're welcome honey bunny.

We talked for a moment. I said The Masseuse was kind of fucking up but I was giving a COVID grace time. The horny Chef said I was amazing. Period. He said I was sweet and he wanted to suck my titties.

He is a fuckboy, a nice one but that is all he is. Neither of us wanted anything else from that so there was no pressure whatsoever. He was very fun though. I wouldn't be seeing him, not in a quarantine. The Poet, yes, because I'm betting he is like me and seeing no one whereas The Chef is probably nailing anyone who will see him. I ain't stupid.

Endings

April 2020

Ups & downs, highs and lows... the quarantine makes everything bigger. I spent Sunday afternoon with The Masseuse. We talked a bit, had amazing sex, and watched *Ozark*. He said he needed Sunday night to get in chill mode for the work week. While I completely respect that, I also thought of merely two weeks ago when he was so excited for me to come over on a Sunday night after he'd had his kids.

I saw he was getting antsy and asked him about it. He said he was thinking of all the things he needed to do. I asked what. Dust, laundry, cook dinner. I'd been there two hours; that's all I'd seen him in seven days and he was thinking about dusting.

That hit me hard. He noticed so we paused the show and talked for 40 minutes about things. I told him how the first two weeks had gone with him wanting to see me and then bam a week ago it was all different and I at first thought he was messing with me but figured out he wasn't. He shook his head and said of course he wasn't. I told him some men like to do that but I could see he was dealing with the weirdness at work, with his kids, with his ex, and his mom.

I told him I wasn't trying to change him at all but I was seeing what he needed and considering what I needed out of a relationship and considering if they meshed. He seemed to understand. I felt really close to him. I told him that although I really like who he is, it might not mean we are compatible for what we want out of life. And that I was trying to figure that out. I thought it was a great talk and felt really good about us when it was over.

Then I fucked up this morning and let needy girl out for a minute and we've had a texting tiff.

You see he didn't text good morning. And he has 85% of the days since I've met him, texted good morning that is. So I texted good morning and he said it back. All fine until I asked what was wrong and he said, *Nothing what do you mean? Just Monday morning busy.* I sent a kiss. He said, *What did I do or not do?*

Damn it.

I said it was silly but he usually texted good morning and I wondered if he was having a stressful morning. He said to take it easy that I was reading into every action or non-action.

Yes, that is what I am doing. I'm losing my shit being home all the time even though I have work to do and moving. I'm extra sensitive and needy from the world situation now. I said sorry, too much time at home. He said that would do it and to quit over-thinking shit with an "lol." I said I'd try and then asked if it were the pot calling the kettle black (because he overthinks too). He said it takes one to know one. I said LOL.

He said I was fine when I left and asked what

happened?

I said I had a great metaphor and could tell him about it tonight. Told him I had done my spinning anxiety thing that I do but that I was fine.

Then he kind of lost his shit.

Another deep and meaningful? he asked.

I thought, fuck, fuck, fuck.

Seriously. It's a lot to keep on discussing and discussing.

Hmmm is it? I asked, a little pissed already.

Kind of...

I like to figure my shit out. It isn't anything bad on you at all or me.

I have a lot to think about... as you mentioned.. I feel like I'm continually worrying about us and if you're ok or not.

Just an observation of how I've been approaching this.

Now I'm doing it here at work when I need to be working.

I'm ok.

Uh huh.

I am.

Doesn't seem like it. When I don't send the text you feel like I should have sent at 6 am.. it wasn't lovey enough ... it stresses me out and I want to withdraw.

Fuck, fuck, fuck. I was hating all of this conversation and wished I'd kept my goddamn needy mouth shut. Damnit to hell. My fault on that. But his on this next part?

I said, *Sorry. I've given you grace through some not fun stuff over the last week. Can you give me some? We really shouldn't text this stuff cuz texting sucks. I really was checking to see if you were okay this morning. Get back to work and don't worry about me lol. I'm fine honey buns. No serious talk tonight. Not needed.*

He didn't even read it I don't think.

It's like we talked for an hour and you were fine we were fine now we need to set up another talk tonight.

No darling, I was just gonna tell you a funny story.

And to be honest we discussed all this yesterday and I don't want to discuss it again the very next day.

He was spinning on things that weren't even there.

I'm kind of maxed, he said.

I texted his name.

Ugh yes? I'm feeling overwhelmed by it. Yeah, he said Ugh.

I asked him to call me so we could talk instead of text it.

He said... *Oh Jesus.*

I said he didn't have to.

He said, *Now I feel fucking bad because of that. Cause you're crying. I'm sorry I think I make you cry.*

I wasn't crying.

It's bullshit how he texts. It is. No excuse. I am aware.

xoxox

Enough is enough. The Masseuse didn't call. That gave me the push to stop this train, for now at least. I didn't say anything the rest of the day, neither did he until after work. He texted and asked if I was alright. I said yes. He said he'd call later.

He didn't.

It's strange to think that as of 5:30 Monday I was going to talk to him on the phone. I would see him Wednesday night here for dinner (if he didn't cancel), I'd go see him Saturday night.

But he didn't call.

As those hours marched by I felt strong. I wasn't upset. I thought he'd call but then as the magic hour of 10 marched closer I realized he wasn't going to.

I called my sister to talk. I was giving it another week.

And then I wasn't. Then I was just done.

I was done with the feeling of waiting for the crumbs of attention from the last week, done with feeling not cherished, done not asking for what I needed at the same time consistently trying to give what he needed.

Done done done.

It was as much about me and how I was feeling as how he was acting. I knew it was time for it to end. He doesn't have room for me and the pandemic in his emotional bandwidth right now. Let's be honest, he may not have room even without the pandemic. It may just be the way he communicates. I am not myself. How can I be? I am more needy, closer to tears at the drop of a hat, needing comfort, a calm listening ear. He doesn't have that. He never did.

Four days in I told him I wasn't coming over because I was worried I could have been exposed to COVID and his children would be coming to his home not 24 hours later. He was not gracious about it. I believe he saw it as some sort of rejection. He texted his annoyance in a harsh manner. Red flag number one was thrown and I stepped over it because our first two dates had been so wonderful. I saw it as an anomaly.

I don't believe it is now. I asked another COVID question about his ex and his work and another awful text convo ensued. I tried to call to talk about it and he denied the call saying he was busy. Red flag number two was not being willing to talk when texting wasn't working. And texting for sure did not work.

He kept backing away and I kept reaching out.

Another weird moment was on Sunday. Hearing the pressure to dust and do laundry while I'm sitting next to him for the first time in a week was devastating. He'd been alone every night, could throw a load of laundry in while children were running around, there was no reason he needed to do that stuff right then. None. Except that he wanted to. I asked what was for dinner and he said that would be part of his chill mode, cooking for himself. In other words get the fuck out. He did apologize for this. He apologized all the time. That kept me going. Hey he knew it wasn't cool so that's the first step to changing it right? Eh. I don't know.

It was a perfect storm wasn't it? His withdrawal coming at a time when I was fully immersed in the relationship, already having developed serious feelings for him and needs. Needs he cannot meet. Needs that aren't even fair to ask this early on.

But what is fair is meeting the challenge of the thing head on together. I think.

Fuck I don't know.

What I do know is I didn't like the feelings I had. I didn't like that he was at the point where he couldn't call me or at least text good night.

He left me hanging. So I cut myself down and walked away.

xoxoxo

The Masseuse looked so good to me, and to my credit those first two dates were simply amazing. I have this cheesy romantic soul and they fed right into it. I saw a survivor who championed me, was compatible in the bedroom, who listened to NPR upon waking. All those things are cool. So cool that I ignored the way he went off the deep end and wouldn't talk to me when we had a conflict. This was the pattern that broke it.

I kept on with him because I know that no relationship is perfect, no human is perfect. There will be something or things that you have to "deal with." That was my thought process.

Although I found it mesmerizing, he used the dark, broody stuff to say I could do better. And that's where I got to. I could. I was consistently telling him he was worthy and he is. I told someone that I thought if he could feel safe with me that stuff would go away. I was letting the bullshit romantic movie 15-year-old who still lives inside me run things. She has never done us any good honestly. She needs to be quiet and go sit in the corner and let mature Scarlett make the decisions.

I did that thing where my mentoring self takes over. I can fix this. I can make this situation better. It is such a pull for me. God I hope that comes out of a good place rather than some egotistical bullshit where I'm everyone's savior. I don't think it is. I want to make the world a better place no matter where I am or who I'm with. But once again I'm learning that my partner needs to be whole already. I'm whole. He must be whole.

My daughters were upset with me because I left the door open with The Masseuse, told him I'd go on a "regular" date if he wanted to when things are better in the world. He said ok. I don't think he will ask honestly. I would go though. Is that stupid?

You know funny thing but maybe not so funny. I validated him through the last convo and all he said was ok and yeah. But perhaps it is too much to ask to receive that back. He wasn't in a place to do it the last few weeks. Why would he be when I'm walking away?

xoxoxo

The cold of the concrete penetrated the knees of my leggings, but my mind was currently with my mouth pleasuring The Hot Chef. I had called him to jump my car. AAA wasn't doing house calls. The Hot Chef was the only person I knew who'd come help me, and come he did.

Before heading to the garage, we had first jumped each other in my loft. The Hot Chef always provided a combo meal of sensuality and physicality for a rousing good time. After I'd come several times and he once, we leaned back against my headboard to catch our breath. Post-coital bliss coursing through our bodies, he handed this marijuana neophyte a weed vape, not telling me how strong it was and I was too dumb to ask. Fully baked we'd strolled to the parking garage and cabled his car to mine. I tried to start my car but nothing happened. We waited, assuming the battery was dead dead, not just half dead. My Honda had honked twice before going into anti-theft mode shutting everything down. It was never going to start as I was supposed to click the fob in a certain pattern, but we didn't know that.

While we waited, we were talking and laughing, attempting to start my car every few minutes, but it wasn't long before we started making out. His lips were soft, meeting mine in sexy symmetry. He pulled my hair and deepened the kiss; our bodies pressed together already heating up, even though we'd just enjoyed each other not a half hour before. He unzipped my jacket, put his hand under my t-shirt, then pinched my nipple in exquisite pain-pleasure. I arched my back wanting to feel him inside me again. Instead I went to my knees, unzipped his jeans, and took him in my mouth. The Hot Chef had a perfect dick. Full, erect, a Goldilocks kind of dick, not too big, not too wide, just right. I wasn't worried about being seen as I was in between two cars.

The late afternoon sun sliced through the parking garage making a halo of light around The Hot Chef's unruly curls. His eyes were closed, hands loosely tangled in my hair. The hard concrete penetrated the knees of my leggings, but I barely noticed as my thoughts were currently with my mouth. A moan escaped The Hot Chef's lips. He leaned back against my car as I ran my tongue up the back of his shaft with some pressure, swirled and teased, then plunged downward to take all of him in my mouth.

He pulled me back up for another make-out session. After a frantic but successful condom search, the ever-prepared Chef walked me a few steps over to his car and bent me over the hood. It must be said: the Hot Chef was delicious. I leaned all the way over so he could get a good angle. He was about five pumps in when the blood, heretofore in other parts of my body, came rushing back into my brain. It screamed at me to stop, that someone could walk out of the loft entryway mere feet away and that… oh god… there were security cameras everywhere.

I stood up and just got my yoga pants pulled over my ass when an older woman walked out of the building. She stared at us as she walked by. I was waiting for her to shame me, throw a stone, yell slut or something. I made myself speak to her about trying to get my car started. She said something innocuous in response, so I was pretty sure she hadn't seen us or at least she wasn't going to make a scene about it. We gave up on starting the car. He rushed off, not seeming to be worried at all about how I'd get the car going. No "I'll check on you later," or anything. He was a fuckboy, not here for the day–to-day details of life like dead cars in parking garages.

I walked back to my loft. My thoughts were like little fish darting away as I tried to catch them to see what I should do about my car and what else I had planned to accomplish that day. I was ravenous so I ate some leftover pizza, then a tiredness blanketed me. Even though it was early evening I crawled under the covers with no energy for the normal nightly rituals of brushing teeth and skin care. At 1:18 a.m. I sat straight up in bed, reality punching me square in the face. I was going to be arrested. I needed to be ready. I turned on all the lights then rifled frantically through my closet. Would the po-po be nicer because they liked my shirt? Maybe? Just in case it mattered I grabbed my new Chiefs Super Bowl shirt, the good sweats (stretchiness so I could bend over to get in the squad car), socks, tennis shoes. I set everything on the floor by the bed for quick access. Should I get my coat? Good god, get a grip, girl. It's not like you killed someone. There will be time to grab your coat. I climbed back in bed to wait.

My thoughts churned around the events of the day that had brought me to this moment. What images could be seen on the camera? The blow-job? Maybe not with the protection of the cars. But my naked ass being railed as I bent over his car? There's no way that wasn't on camera. I thought about walking out to the parking garage right then to see where the cameras were but it was cold and dark and what did it matter at this point?

Would the police come now or in the morning? Probably morning. No one would see the video evidence before that. Wait though, what if someone was watching the cameras 24/7? Then they could be here any minute! I'd be fired. I only needed three more years of teaching to retire.

Lights ablaze, I sat in bed staring at the ashes of my life.

Ding!

A text popped up from my 26-year-old middle daughter who'd just finished her bartending shift. She would have words of advice for me. My kids and I openly talked to each other about our lives. I called to tell her what happened and to ask if I'd be arrested. She kindly explained I was paranoid from the pot and everything would be okay.

I now knew why, even though The Hot Chef was a sweetheart, something about him scared me. He was wild as a March hare and I felt a bit uncool if I didn't follow along.

It was time to take a break from men.

xoxoxo

The year of sluttery was a very purposeful journey:
• To date many men but not have a relationship,
• To have lots of sex but not catch feelings,
• To just have some fun already.
   How did it go?
   Overall fairly excellent really.

I was always safe. I followed my heart. I learned so much. I had so much fun.

But it hasn't been as fun lately. I'm ready for something different.

First of all, a man sabbatical. I started on a course a year ago. And have arrived at a different place. As I look back at the last few months several things show me I need to recalibrate.

I've been working on having a voice. I should have kicked Zen Man's ass to the curb in an Uber when he was high and drunk instead of appeasing him with sex. I should have asked The Writer why he couldn't get his face out of a computer screen when we were on our virtual "date" instead of trying to be more interesting. I should have stuck to my guns to not see The Masseuse when I didn't want to the first week. I went and it was awkward. I became needy girl with him and lost my balance. I should have said no to The Chef instead of going along even if it was fun for a minute then it wasn't. In all of these circumstances I did things I didn't really want to. I fell too fast (well not The Chef, he's an FWB) but the others I kinda made a fool of myself by seeing something interesting and making up a picture of them that wasn't true. I just filled in all the details I didn't know yet instead of being patient and seeing what's up. I am rounding up and instead I need to round down. That makes so much sense to me.

I was on a fuck mission since September but tried to switch gears the last few months without pushing in the clutch. I was beginning to be open to the idea of one man but I was attacking it like it needed to happen NOW. Fill the expectations NOW. In other words, although I've learned so much about myself and am listening more to Pussy, my inner wisdom, I still have a journey to go on of being whole on my own. I'm trying too hard and moving too fast to fill something in me.

This ship was headed one way and has seen that coast. I thought I knew which way to head and steamed forward only to get grounded. I got unstuck and am setting the anchor to float for a while. See where I want to go next.

I know that involves putting my money where my mouth is in several ways that I say matter to me but have chosen the dating apps & men over them. These include getting out in nature more through camping, hiking, biking, and kayaking; developing closer relationships with my friends and family; building new ones by forming that female tribe; writing and getting published in areas I haven't; researching my next steps after retirement; creating a meditation and yoga practice; building strength and health; starting a podcast... that's it for now I guess.

I'm scared as shit but the anchor is down. I'm floating. I may fuck up but I will try my best.

We'll see what happens. Will it be monogamous dating? Will it be only FWBs, no dating? Maybe I'll even go for the Year of Sluttery take two. Will I be poly? I don't know.

Recalibration begins now bitches (and I say that in the most loving way).

xoxoxo

How are you feeling? Miss you, The Masseuse texted. He had texted the week before to tell me he went to get a COVID blood test at the doctor and it was negative for antibodies which made him feel better. Now that I was a week out from the break-up I saw how the quarantine hit me so hard and pushed this connection with a stranger. I told him this.

He said, *It is just your attention is now distracted by 'the others' lol. No need to apologize.*

I'm not dating anyone, silly head.

I know but the other casuals.

I had told him about my year of sluttery and even said the words "fuckboys" to him, which had shocked him.

Nope. Taking a little man sabbatical to figure out my shit, I responded.

Oh.

Then I said I missed him. I wish I hadn't said that. I do miss being with him but I don't miss the other stuff. I think there's too much shit for anything to work so I really need to cut and go, like I already did. He did have some really great qualities but I'm not listening to Pussy am I? Damnit to hell, no I'm not.

He responded with, *Well maybe sometime we can share a meal and a movie.*

Yes let's.

Ok. So I'm not included in your man sabbatical?

You didn't say a day so I figured when my man-battical is over May 19. I set a month at minimum. I'm moving anyway and will be busy the next few weeks.

Oh so I'm making a date to see you in a month?? I could be dead! Then he said, *Ok well then tonight's out eh*

Little asshole was texting a booty call at 4:15 in the afternoon but couching it in a "Sometime we can do a movie and dinner?"

I said, *You were texting to ask me out tonight? I thought you were teasing me lol. I need a bit of a heads up for one but I also still have grad classes.*

Ok well maybe in a month lol.

Maybe. I should have left it at this but did I? Of course not. *If you want... If you still miss me*

Ok I'm sure I will.

Hold on. Pussy is trying to tell me something, "But it's not enough honey. It's just not enough. And you aren't a bad person because it's not enough. It doesn't mean he isn't a great person if you walk away because it's not right for you. You don't need to make everyone's life better. Your students, your friends and family, yes. Men. No. You don't have to do that. I know you want to love everyone. You have all this love and care but you aren't the hospital for broken men. It takes you away from what you are supposed to be doing, what you want to be doing. You aren't his savior. He can get counseling. He can do meditation. He can figure his shit out without you. Yes he's a lovable little cuss with a dry sense of humor and that dimple in his chin but he ain't for you right now. He's not whole. You need whole."

Yeah you are right Pussy. So I shouldn't be texting

something I walked away from. Fuck fuck fuck. Okay it's all okay. I already said I wasn't going to see him for a month, at least. I haven't made any commitments. Just drop it. Move on.

Here this will help me, even just to write it and not send it: Masseuse I am setting you free. I see so many qualities in you that show me we could have been something cool. You are valuable. You are a hero to me in fact for who you are, where you've come from, the strength you've shown, the courage, the drive to succeed. I admire you. You don't have what I need though and I have to take care of me. I'm sorry I gave mixed signals. I am a human and confused sometimes. Me walking away does not mean you do not have worth. Not at all. It's just not the right thing for either of us. There will just be pain I think. Go work on you. I'm gonna work on me. Peace babe.

xoxoxo

I was supposed to move this weekend to a studio apartment in the most gorgeous old building. Then Saturday I woke up and thought, I don't want to do it. It's the quarantine bitches. Life may never be the same as it was.

I can't think that way too long or I just want to go to bed and cry so let's just look at the next year. It ain't going to be the same. Living in a loft downtown is cool when I can go to coffee shops to write, visit the library rooftop garden, go out for drinks at different establishments several times a week. But this life, sitting in a tiny space looking out a window that doesn't open, no balcony, no outdoor space to work. I need out.

I need air and sun and space. I did an online rental home search, gathered a list of nine places that were safe and in my budget and headed out to drive past them. The first five were awful. I drove down to the fifth house. Fell in love with this place the minute I stepped in. Hardwood floors, archways, black and white tile in the kitchen, and best of all a front porch. I have always always wanted to have a front porch. I have never in my life had a front porch. I'm moving there next Wednesday. Except for the whole "no one will help me move" moment of despair, this joy that bubbled up in me. I can make a french boudoir out of that little room by the bathroom. I can put my wicker chair on the front porch. I can put my writing desk in the dining room because there is great light there. I'll get plants. The hammock can go in my backyard.

I moved downtown last year and have adored it. I love this city. Everyday on the way to teach in the 'burbs I blew the Kansas City skyline a kiss and told her I loved her and I'd be back later. I may come back to live downtown but honestly I don't think I will. I think I can enjoy the new house and journey the sixty blocks to enjoy downtown.

I'm ready for this little house, more peace and quiet.

xoxoxo

The dream house that Hoppy and I bought together in 2017 has sold. He has to be out next week. When I moved away a year ago I left some shit there because he didn't care. He was alone in a four-bedroom home. I was moving to a loft. It made sense.

Now he's moving and it was time to take care of that shit so I've been there the last two Saturdays in a row. We talked quite a bit, even sat on the deck after I had worked for three hours. I can see why I fell so hard for him at the same time as I can see why we aren't meant to be together.

I fell for him because he is to his core a kind and good person. His first inclination is to help someone out. He knows how to take care of shit. He came over a few weeks ago to help me get my car jumped when The Chef wasn't able to the night before. When the car just shut down he told me to Google it, lo and behold there's a theft system. He's so smart like that. When I was there to pack, he had boxes and tape and paper for me to use, extra that he didn't need. He was someone I could always lean on and did. For the first time in my adult life when I was with him, I was able to let go of being in charge of so many things and let him do it. He paid for so many things for us, paid the house payment for many months even though I was supposed to be paying half but I was getting facials since he's ten years younger than I am.

I feel so comfortable with him. He's funny and makes me laugh. We had a lot of fun together. Some of my favorite memories of him were:

- going to St. Louis for NYE for a nice dinner then concert then breakfast, staying in bed in the luxury hotel the whole next day except to walk to get food.
- tormenting him in the grocery store kissing him.
- going to Blues games, especially when I saw a hat trick.
- going to Jamaica with him the first time.
- when he surprised me with my first Easter basket in my whole life

However, I leaned on him too much. It became a problem with him that he didn't talk about to me. He did not know how to work through conflicts which is ultimately what killed the relationship. I'd bring something up, even tell him ahead so he could mull it, and then we'd talk and he'd get so upset and couldn't just let of the idea that I might not be happy so he'd cave and then I'd be mad because I didn't want him to cave. I wanted to work it out, to get down to the nitty gritty and figure it out. He couldn't do it. He'd get so upset and just walk away. That's why I asked for couple counseling thinking we could learn that together but he quit going after the second session. Another problem was we were not compatible in the bedroom as my drive is way higher than his. No judgement there, everyone has their sweet spot.

The last thing that wasn't good is that I stopped doing my stuff to sit by him on the couch. I didn't write at all, hardly read, just sat by him watching TV. That is not how I want to spend my life. He never told me to do that but I knew he'd like me to be there and I wanted to please him.

I think he is just now processing some of the breakup as he moves from the home we bought together. Having spent so much time with him this week, I'm 1000% percent over him. I never wanted to get back with him but still loved him a little. I only love him as a friend now. I want the very best for him, offered again to help him set up his dating profile. He turned me down again.

He came over to get some boxes that I was done with and saw my new place and I think it bothered him a little. He's never once said he missed me or tried to kiss me or been flirty. Not once. That is some strength as he didn't want me to go.

xoxoxo

Put a fork in it. I'm done. The year of sluttery is over. Now this scares the hell out of me to say that. But I know it in my woman wisdom. Tomorrow it will be a full year of being single. I named it The Year of

Sluttery. I have taken from it what I needed. I am glad I did it.

I went from a 28-year-marriage to the relationship with Hoppy after two months. I went from Hoppy to the dating apps in 48 hours. I've learned so much. I know in my bones to continue is not what I need. When I think of no sluttery, the fear is right there again. But why?

Say I take these hours and pour them into myself and then decide I am poly. Well that's good. Then I will know my journey. I don't think that will happen. I think I want a deep connection with one man someday, mentally, physically, emotionally, and spiritually. A connection that feeds both of us, allows us to truly be ourselves and in fact champions that. A relationship of cherishing, laughter, joy, and shenanigans. See that feels really good to write that.

I need a year for me. I am scared to write this. I am scared to even think it but I am saying it because it is truth. Who am I without the stories, the craziness of different men, the hours of messaging, looking forward to the next date? I have learned about what I want and what I deserve. Now it is time to focus all those hours on my journey as a person, to walk away from the easy distraction of the apps, the compliments, the attention.

To look fully into the abyss of solitude and loneliness and see who I am. To take those hours and develop myself, my projects, relationships with friends, see who I want to be and need to be in the next stage of life. I'm not saying there will be no men in The Year of Discovery. I'm saying I don't know how or what or when that might be. I just know I need to honor my journey and stop this train for now.

xoxoxo

April 19, 2020
Dear One Year Ago Scarlett,
Damn girl you are gonna learn so much about yourself this year.

You learn not to apologize for your body, for the stomach roll and the cellulite on your thighs. You've not only had no complaints when those thighs are wrapped around someone but Men love your bootie; and those boobs you were worried about because they fed three babies? Oh no, hell to the nah. They are beloved by the menz. Also they like to pull your hair.

Secondly and these are not in order of importance because this one is MORE important than physical beauty, you learn about your true feminine powers from *Women Who Run With the Wolves* by Dr. Clarissa Pinkola-Estes who is now rockstar status in your world. Then you read *Pussy: A Reclamation* and it moved you even more forward in listening to your pussy, yeah that's what I said. In this bullshit patriarchal society women's moods, emotions, and intuition are incessantly mocked. We are rising though. Women are supporting each other, knowing their power. Change is coming.

You listen to your intuition and get better at walking away from men quicker. You thought that if a man is good, he is good for you. Nope. You realize that you build a persona around them, "rounding them up" in the words of a friend. You are open and that is okay and that is good darling.

This "Okayness" with yourself is another thing you've learned. You've always put yourself down for these feelings, for being so much. You are almost there, a year later, almost to the point where you honor who you are fully. You are even learning to be okay with the bullshit about yourself, to understand it and not shame yourself. This one is hard and still in process and that's okay.

You learned you are bold and can make most men shake in their boots if you want to. You don't....much, well the parts they like and you do, the seduction, mmmmm. You love to feel your power to turn men on. You learned how very much you like sex. You had no idea did you? Well girl, you really like it. And now you've been with enough lovers you know what you want and that's good.

Damn girl, you are in for quite an adventure. Have fun darling. See you on the flip side. As for me, I'm heading on to The Year of Discovery.

What does that mean? Whatever the fuck I want it to mean.

A PEEK AT

The Year of Discovery

The Forklift Driver mentioned he's met someone. And of course that's wonderful. I want everyone to find their person and if it ain't me, it ain't me. That's the logical side speaking.

The emotional side was really sad. I examined this sadness. I felt stupid about it because it's "dumb" to feel sad over a two-week flirty email penpal sitch. I felt rejected although the brain was telling me I'm not. I mean, yes it is rejection in its simplest form. The Forklift Driver was so nice to say we could still email but the "tone" would be different. Well duh. We were telling sexy stories and I may have sent a photo, or two. So a rejection of the lover but not the budding friendship.

I feel embarrassed that I sent the photos now. Finding a balance here is hard for me. I want be honest and be who I am in that moment and place and so I communicate from that place and try to honor it but then I get embarrassed when I don't "win." I didn't win. I lost. I tried too hard that voice says.

The thing is he was accepting of all of it and said,

"nothing is too much." And I don't think it was. I don't think any of this is in any form a rejection of me. It is simply the way things happened.

I know this is dramatic. I'm struggling even writing about it. It's shameful to me to have these feelings. I'm doing it to love that part of me too. Or trying to.

I battled the feeling of stupidity from a voice saying, "He hasn't been writing. You should have known something was up but oh no you still were thinking you mattered to him." The other really embarrassing feeling was one I hate and don't agree with but it's there floating around, "You aren't good enough." That's not true. I am. But that little idea goes flying through on a banner behind the plane. I see it, I don't believe that but why does it show up? Perhaps this shows up for everyone? I think it does.

I watched myself inside as all this came up and I teared up but didn't let myself get too emotional, was proud I was battling that emotion. But it was there, this sadness, so I shoved it down last night and then shoved it down this morning and then told my writing group about it.

I heard, "Don't trash yourself for having a need."

And "The antidote is love and compassion instead of trying to get rid of it. Love that part of you. Hold and feel it and appreciate your tender heart."

Wait what? I get to accept the parts of me I'm not proud of? The squishy ridiculous emotional side?

"Love those wounded pieces, just as you do with others."

"Practice being in the knowing rather than the confusion."

"Walk through the 'shameful' messages that live inside to get back."

"Home is in us. Feel. it," they said.

So here I am, still feeling a bit sad about the idea of what might have been with the Forklift Driver, feeling full love and acceptance from my friends this morning, walking through the voices that aren't truth but are there and trying to love that weak thing inside me.

Trying. I don't like her yet. But maybe I can love her?

Home is in me. I offer this love and compassion to others; why not myself? It is so odd to write that. The image came to me of a fish out of water trying to breathe. The water is home. I have been thrown on the shore and I'm struggling for breath, for oxygen. The water is love, is self-acceptance, whole and surrounding me if I will let it. If I will throw myself back in, again and again, and acknowledge it is whole and perfect and enough.

I am whole and perfect and enough. Home is in me.

ABOUT THE AUTHOR

Hello sweet reader,

I began writing about my year of sluttery on a blog back in 2019. In 2020 I realized this could be a book, pulled all the posts from the year and began the five year journey of working on this damn thing.

I retired from teaching, the reason I had taken the name Scarlett, but chose to keep a pseudonym since my parents don't even know about this. (Would you tell your parents if you wrote a book like this? I didn't think so.) And I was trying to be nice to my kids who, let's be honest, have been through enough with all my shenanigans.

I was going to go through the excruciating steps to get an agent and publisher after receiving 35 rejections, and reworking the whole book, and then one day I decided not to. I decided to just get it out there.

So here it is.

Thank you for reading it.

XOXOXO
Scarlett

Scarlett is a bit nomadic right now, maybe coming to a town near you for a book reading or Fringe Fest. You can stay tuned at scarlettdjones.com